W9-CJP-743

265144

DATE DUE

AUG 2 9	
JUN 3 0 2004	

HOW TO BUILD
A TIN CANOE

HOW TO BUILD
A TIN CANOE
Confessions of an Old Salt

R O B B   W H I T E

NEW YORK

DISCLAIMER

None of these stories is true . . . not a single word. If you think you recognize yourself in any of these fictitious characters I talk so bad about, that's just your own paranoia. There is no point in suing me anyway. Because of the nature of the boat-building business, I don't own anything at all, and if you decide to take it out on my ass, just remember, you got to bring some to get some.

Copyright © 2003 by Robb White

All rights reserved. No part of this book may be used or reproduced in any manner whatsoever without the written permission of the Publisher. Printed in the United States of America. For information address Hyperion, 77 West 66th Street, New York, New York 10023-6298.

Library of Congress Cataloging-in-Publication Data

White, Robb.
    How to build a tin canoe : confessions of an old salt / Robb White.—1st ed.
      p. cm.
    ISBN 1-4013-0027-8
    1. White, Robb, 1941– 2. Boatbuilders—Georgia—Biography.
  3. Boatbuilders—Florida—Biography. I. Title.

VM140.W497A3 2003
623.8'2'092—dc21
[B]

                                        2002192173

Hyperion books are available for special promotions and premiums. For details contact Hyperion Special Markets, 77 West 66th Street, 11th floor, New York, New York 10023, or call 212-456-0133.

FIRST EDITION

10 9 8 7 6 5 4 3 2 1

This book is dedicated to my wife, Jane. If you manage to struggle all the way through it, you'll understand why.

CONTENTS

The Boat in the Coach House   1
in which I sink as far as possible

The Tin Canoe of World War Two   9
in which I begin a lifetime of building eyeball designed boats

The Reynolds   18
*in which I learn the true meaning of life . . . when I am
young enough to make some good use of the knowledge*

The Reynolds Crew Discovers St. George Island   26
and saves the day with a brave rescue

Another Reynolds Rescue 43
*in which I escape formal education but
become educated nevertheless*

A Few Recipes of the Reynolds Crew 53
in which I begin a lifetime as a gourmet

Sailfish 62
in which someone else learns a lesson . . . well, almost

Storm Boat Motor 68
*in which, due to the onset of puberty, I foolishly expand
my compulsion to include machinery*

How I Became a Boatbuilder 74
*in which I take a wife, turn professional,
and learn a lot all at the same time*

Terrible Torque and the Floorboard Man 88
*in which there is a terrible tragedy,
so you might want to skip this one*

Monkey Island 97
in which I leave my young bride for . . . monkeys

Seagull 104
in which I learn not to be so gullible

Prams 111
in which I become a successful, professional boatbuilder
first shot out of the box

Pleistocene Creek 115
in which I almost give it all up and quit the
boatbuilding business for good

Sheephead Head Soup 123
in which there are the natural histories of two fish
and a worm and . . . yet another recipe

Sea Turtle 134
in which I learn my lesson about being so presumptuous . . .
well, almost

Cobio 138
in which I save my children from starvation
but almost freeze to death in the process

The Giant Catfish of Mobile 148
in which I meet an astonishing transvestite . . .
and cook breakfast

King Tut 155
in which I prove the disclaimer that none of these stories
could possibly be true

The Slave's Recipe 158
in which I do a little more tugging, get involved in a criminal
conspiracy, and get locked up for murder . . . and learn a new
recipe . . . and satisfy a lifelong curiosity . . . a long story

Islands   174
in which I reveal yet another obsession

The Canned Ham Incident   179
in which I do not participate, so Hurrah for the other side

Dead Man's Boat   190
in which I reveal two morals

The Old J 80 Johnson   196
in which I help a man recover his long-lost self-esteem

The Sailing, Commercial Fishing Felucca "Bullet" # 9999   200
in which there is a poem

The Caribs and the Arawaks   215
in which I figure out economics, but too late to participate
in any of it

An Analog Mind Stuck in a Digital World   219
in which I finally, in the twilight of my life, figure out what
the hell is wrong with me and effect a complete cure

Cooking Up Opinions   224
in which I finally set aside my peculiar ways and
start acting like all the other old men in the world

Acknowledgments   227

HOW TO BUILD
A TIN CANOE

THE BOAT IN THE COACH HOUSE

in which I sink as far as possible

I REMEMBER MY FIRST BOAT. I had been in other boats ever since I was a little baby, but the boat in the coach house was the first one to belong to me and, you know, that makes a lot of difference. I think I was about four or five years old when I became a boat owner for the first time.

There were two segments of our family, the wild and the civilized. My family was the former. While my father and uncles were off attending to WWII, my grandfather, my mother, me, a bunch of aunts, and all sorts of folks who worked the old place were all that was left of the wild segment of our family. My grandfather was an unusual man. Though he was capable of doing anything useful and was loved and respected by everybody who knew him, he was incompetent in the management of money (sort of like me, I guess). I believe that he suffered from excess enthusiasm. If he had been in a primitive situation—something like an old savage sitting around his fire, roasting little morsels of meat on a stick for his grandchildren—he would have been fine, but he just didn't fit in the modern world (never learned to drive a car, for one thing).

The other segment of our family was connected to my grandfather's sister, who, along with her husband, was a rich Yankee. Our place (12,000 acres then) was what they call a "hunting plantation." Which, I believe, are maintained by rich Yankees as a winter refuge from the rigors of piling up money and as a tax dodge. There were, and are, a bunch of them around here. This is longleaf pine country, and those kinds of woods were thought to be "salubrious" back when people were scared to death of things like tuberculosis, so the industrial tycoons of the late nineteenth century started coming here for their health right after the Civil War. There were hotels in Thomasville, Georgia, that catered to them, and when my grandfather's grandfather first started coming down here for extended vacations in the winter they stayed in a fancy hotel (the Piney Woods), then they built a house in town . . . then, in 1886, they bought the old Blackshear place down on the Florida line and started vacating in the real piney woods.

My grandfather had been a rich Yankee, too, but he loved roaming through the woods and messing around in the water down here so much that he never went back to Philadelphia to tend to his business, and it dwindled to nothing even before the crash of '29. He worked for his sister as overseer of the plantation. His four children ran the woods like coons all the time. There was a tutor who lived on the place and was supposed to teach them the three R's, but they were so bright and eager to get out that all formal education was accomplished before breakfast. These children quickly reverted to "wild type," like the escaped fruit flies in a genetics lab. The deformities of civilization evaporated from them like the ether used to knock out the special flies that lived with their birth defects in jars in the lab. One story is that if they found a shutbox (eastern box turtle, *Terrapene carolina*) while they were wandering the woods, they immediately raked up a pile of pine straw, set it on fire, and put the turtle in there to roast. If he (or she—a he has red eyes) crawled out, they raked him back in with a stick. He was done when the steam began to come out from under his tail, and they busted him open and ate him on the spot. My mother, who was the Red Cross lady in Thomasville for many years, was such a nice person that nobody ever suspected the depths of her savagery. She was never sick a day in her life and attributed that to the early challenges to her immune system.

Anyhow, these wild, savage children were extremely cruel to the tame little Yankee cousins when they came down. I mean, goddamighty knows, some of those stories will curdle the blood. I'll quickly whip out two so you can see what I mean, but I'll try to spare you all I can. One time, they hung a little innocent boy by his belt onto the horns of a deer skull nailed to the wall of the coach house. It wasn't child abuse . . . at first. He was willing, but an airplane flew over about then (1918), and they had to run see and forgot the little fella until they noticed his empty place at supper time. Another time, they told the whole crew of innocents that when you chewed sugarcane, you were supposed to swallow the pummins. I better explain that or it might not be as impressive to people who have never chewed cane. There are three components: First there is the peeling, which is exactly like bamboo—

stuff nobody but a panda can chew. Next there is the juice, which is astonishingly delicious. Unfortunately the juice is soaked up in the pummins, which is just about like a piece of hemp rope. Southerners used to caulk boats with cane pummins. My mother and aunt and uncles had those little gullible Yankees all in a row swallowing like matching cormorants, each with a pinfish trying to go down backward. Jesus. My sisters and I did it to one of our Yankee cousins, too, and it was pitiful. I hope St. Peter is on his break when my time comes, so I can slip by the substitute.

The little wild children didn't have anything much. They made bows and arrows with the single worn-out pocketknife that they shared, and they had a box of matches, a few fish hooks, and a spool of "Aunt Lydia" sewing thread. Later, when they were old enough (about seven), they had a gun. Oh, they ate well, because this was actually a working plantation with big fields of peanuts and a garden from which everybody on the place (maybe thirty people, all told) had all they needed. There was livestock of all kinds: My grandfather raised pigeons for the squabs. You know, a squab is a peculiar phenomenon. When they get ready to kill and eat, they are much bigger than a grown pigeon . . . sort of like how a caterpillar is bigger than the butterfly into which it metamorphoses. They don't actually look all that appetizing with their pin feathers sticking straight out and all that dook stuck on their bottoms because their legs are too flaccid for them to waddle out of it. But, I tell you this, a squab roasted with a strip of bacon is a treat. There are a lot of foodstuffs kind of like that, you know, those that don't look too good as raw material, but with proper preparation, turn out fine. A hot dog is a good example of that. But the point is that the little wild children were well fed but poor.

Well, the little Yankees had all sorts of toys and junk. Everything a child could have was provided for them, not only down here, but back in Philadelphia. Momma said that they had a real steam train, big enough to ride on. Years later she showed me the little rusty tracks running all out through the flower beds over at the big house. They also had a tiny boat.

Everybody in the family was grown up when I, the first of the new generation, came along. My sisters and I and a bunch of children of the folks that worked the place ran just as wild as before. What did you think . . . that someone like my mother would, all of a sudden, fly into a frenzy of supervision? I was the oldest, by far, and for a long time, I was by myself. I was out there in the coach house one time when I found a ladder nailed to the harness wall and, after I had climbed into the loft, I found the most charming little boat.

I'll get right back to it in a second, but first I better explain the coach house. Back in the horse and buggy days, a buggy was an expensive thing and a "coach" was something reserved for people like my ancestors—people who were apt to top it the knob every chance they got. One story is that when they came (I guess my grandfather was a little boy at this time) down for the winter on the "Carpetbagger Express," they would spend the first night in their house in town while their servants got the coach ready. It was big enough to haul them all, all the men in their Prince Alberts and beavers, and all the ladies in their plume-bird hats. There was a little perch up front for the driver, and a little perch back aft for the man who blew the horn to warn the peasants to get out of the way. If that ain't topping it the knob, I don't know what is. I actually knew one old man who remembered those days. He said,

"You heard that horn, you better get your ass out the road or them goddamn Masons would run over you in that big-assed thing." Anyway, the coach house is where the coach stayed so that the mohair and plush and leather wouldn't get rained on. When I was a little boy, it was full of agricultural implements, rusty tools, old harnesses, and some old, dusty buggies and wagons. No telling what happened to the coach and the horn.

So I found that little boat up in the loft with some old fishing poles (we had our own bamboo grove, which is right down in back of my son's house right now—most excellent stuff) and old, dusty lumber. I remember it exactly. During the time of the coach and on up into the thirties, there was a man named Dan Kidney in Ohio who built double-ended duckboats. They were decked over and had an oval cockpit. When I was a boy, there was one in every pond on the place. As with the fancy canoes my Yankee relatives brought down, the duckboats didn't last long down here, and by the time the war was over and I was old enough to make much use of them, they were rotted out. The one in the coach house was a miniature that the Yankees had built specially to suit the needs of their children. Initially, there was a whole fleet of them, but all but one had succumbed to the fecundity of the South. Nobody knew how this one got up in the loft of the coach house, but there it was. It didn't take me long to get it down so I could get to messing. I wasn't even old enough to go to school, but I was old enough to need a boat of my own.

I dragged it to the closest creek and slid it in. The old cedar planking had shrunk and gapped so bad that I couldn't keep it bailed out. When I got in, the bottom spouted like the whales in *McElligot's Pool*. It didn't make any difference in the long run, though, because the creek was too little to float the boat anyway. I fought and dragged it all the way to the delta, where the creek spread out at the head of the pond. There, the button bushes, briers, stagger bushes, and grass were too thick for me to get any farther, and I had to abandon the whole project right there. I guess an archaeologist, armed with sophisticated infrared devices, could find a hint of extra richness in the shape of a tiny boat in the humus of that place. I might fight my way back through the impenetrable thicket myself one of these days with my metal detector and see if I can find one single clenched tack for my artifact cabinet.

Epilogue

When I got out of the Navy in 1963 and set up in the boatbuilding business, all the old Kidney boats on all the Yankee places down here had rotted out. I hate to talk bad about legendary things, but they weren't very well made. When the Yankees found that there was a boatbuilder in town (me—right downtown in an old storefront), one of them asked me if I thought I knew what a Dan Kidney boat looked like and, if so, could I build one? "Will a yellow butterfly light on a dog turd?" was my reply. I surveyed a few wretched scraps at the ponds on our place and found little pieces of galvanized tin, rusty steel nails, little pieces of rotten northern white cedar, and even a little crust of painted canvas. From that, and my childhood memories, I was able to build an ersatz Kidney boat. Abercrombie & Fitch had stopped selling the real thing by then, so I had no competition. The duckboat business was one of the things that lured me into deceiving myself that I could make a living as a boatbuilder. I built a lot of them—saturated the market. The only problem was that I didn't have good business sense like old Dan. Mine were made of old-growth, red-heart cypress fastened with copper and bronze, and they never rotted out. The old boats had two galvanized tin pipes down through the foredecks (they were symmetrically double-ended) and all the way through the bottom so you could stick a pole down into the bottom of the pond to stabilize the boat in the blind. Though the Yankees didn't do much bream fishing, I found that the pipes (mine were copper) were the best way to hold the boat over a bed so rambunctious grandchildren won't turn the boat over when the old redbellies get to biting like they do sometimes. Does that mean that I have one of those boats? Can a fat baby fart?

THE TIN CANOE OF
WORLD WAR TWO

*in which I begin a lifetime of building
eyeball designed boats*

I WAS BORN AND raised in a place called the "Red Hills" region of Georgia. Contrary to the *Tobacco Road* sound of the name, it is so wonderful here that I have never stayed for very long anyplace else. This is the last outpost of the pitifully endangered virgin longleaf pine woods that used to cover the entire coastal plain of the southeastern United States from Virginia to Texas, including all of Florida down to the Everglades. The place in the woods where I grew up down here on the Georgia/Florida line has a bunch of ponds scattered all around, and we kept some kind of old boat or other in each one of them. Usually those boats were the everlasting, immobile, flat-bottomed, rough-sawn, five-quarter cypress style that stayed in the water and full of water and skeeter wigglers all the time. Sometimes somebody would want to use one bad enough to dip the water out and pull the willow trees out of the cracks in the bottom, but most of the time they stayed right where they were and we fished off the bank. I was usually the one who went to all the trouble to make one of the old boats move because I wasn't patient enough to sit in the same place and watch my cork and wait for the fish to come to me. I could see them out there roiling the water beyond the range of my cane pole and I deluded myself that, if I could just get out there, I could catch them.

In addition to all these ponds but out back of the old place, there was a respectable river, one of those meandering kinds with cutoff sloughs all through the woods. Those cutoffs were full of fish and ducks. I yearned for a little lightweight boat that I could carry, all by myself, from one little hole of water to another and even put in the main river when it was navigable. This was back in the days of the wood-canvas canoe, and some of our Yankee cousins brought them down and they were fun while they lasted, but they didn't last very long. The water that got between the canvas and the slats never got a chance to dry out in this humidity and they would grow a crop of mushrooms after about one season unless the boats were carefully dried out in the loft of the barn every time they got used. Such carefulness is not in the nature of my family, and we ruined some beautiful old canoes. When gas got rationed during World War Two, the cousins stopped bringing them down anyway, so I took the roof off my uncle's chicken house operation that he abandoned when he went off to fight and made me a tin canoe. You wouldn't think that the jackleg* efforts

---

Jackleg is a name applied to people who drank so much moonshine that the lead and fusil oil from junkpile stills combined in their brains to disrupt the

of a filthy, dirty, poorly supervised child would turn out to be worth a flip, but even now that I am a serious (well) professional boatbuilder with more than forty years in the business, I seldom build a boat that turns out all that much better than those tin canoes.

The first tin canoes were primitive. Now, they were satisfactory, all right, but they needed improvement. I remember the launching of the very first one as if it happened yesterday. I think it was sixteen feet long and I know it was made of one sheet of what they call "five V-crimp" roofing tin meant to span two feet on the roof of something like a chicken house. I bent the ends of the tin up and nailed it onto two rough cypress two-by-four stems sticking up almost vertical. Though it was caulked with regular, never-get-hard roofing tar, it leaked not only around the stems, but up through the holes where the nails used to be when the tin was still on the chicken house. The tar over the nail holes transferred itself to my skin when I was in the boat and earned me one of my early nicknames, "Spotty." The boat, though, was light and easy to drag by the stem through the bushes. The galvanize seemed to lubricate its bottom (a fact exploited by the airboat builders around here for years until the invention of high-tech) and it slid

---

motor control of at least one leg. The result was an uncontrollable "jacking" of that leg when the poor fool tried to walk. When the jackleg began to affect both legs at the same time, the person fell down and was unable to go get any more moonshine, so the affliction was, in a way, self-limiting. Cruel people began to use "jackleg" as an adjective to describe projects that look like the work you would expect from someone whose brain is in such shape. Often, such observations are the result of the arrogance of jealous people who are too devoted to the imaginary dignity of ignorance and helplessness to have interesting projects of their own. . . . Watch yourself.

over the grass and pond weeds like they weren't even there. I couldn't wait to get in. It took a few tries.

I learned that I had to be careful. The narrow tin made the balance between beam and freeboard real tricky. If I made the boat too narrow, it was so tippy that I couldn't get settled before it turned over. If I made it too wide, it wouldn't have enough freeboard and would sink quickly to the bottom so that soon, the only thing that would be sticking up out of the water would be me and the two stems. There is a remarkable photograph of that in the family album. I'm the one in the middle with the hat.

When I finally managed to get it adjusted so that I could get in and push off, I knew I had something. The tin canoe moved through the water like a snake. Just paddling with my hands would make it sizzle across the pond. I had to be careful not to cut myself on the sharp edges of the tin, and to keep track of the bilge-water situation, but luckily, the first pond was one of the shallow ones and I didn't lose my boat before I trained myself. I was obsessed. The abandoned chicken house had enough tin to make a big fleet of tin canoes and I instantly set out to improve the model. About the time all the men came home from World War Two and stopped all those women from spoiling me, I had evolved the tin canoe into a mighty fine boat.

You Can Build One for Yourself . . .
Here's the Step by Step

The highly evolved five V-crimp tin canoe is built like this. You need a sixteen-foot sheet of tin. Short tin might seem, at first, to be more workable, but we are messing around on the fringes of possible here, and twelve or fourteen feet of tin won't keep you out of the water quite as long as sixteen feet will. After you get your tin home from wherever you got it (that stuff will slide out of a pickup and blow off a car, too), the first thing to do is wash it with strong detergent to get the oil off, then fold it down the middle like a piece of paper. Don't crimp it along the center crimp too bad, just enough to get the tin to come together at the stems. Put some polyurethane adhesive sealant on the one-by-two stems and screw the tin to them with short stainless steel flathead screws. See if you can drive the screws in so they bend the tin into a countersunk place so the heads will be sort of flush and won't catch weeds so bad. It helps to pre-do-it with strong, hardened black steel screws that won't wring off before they get flush. I know it is a lot of trouble, but this is a high performance boat . . . you got to do it right. Don't cut yourself. WD-40 will get that dook off of you if you don't wait too long.

Stomping the Boat Into Shape

This is the tricky part. If you think you have enough screws in both ends, you can go ahead right away and not wait the long time for that polyurethane to set up. My patience hasn't completely developed yet, so I tell myself that it is best if the caulking is still sticky. That way, it will be able to follow the distortion of the tin as the hull is shaped.

Start stomping right in the middle. Bare feet, very gritty, are best, but soft tennis shoes might work okay. Gradually stomp all the deadrise out of the tin in the center of the boat and work it forward and aft by walking and stomping. It is best to do this on soft ground sort of like a nice fluffy lawn. Do it in the backyard so you won't attract too much attention (this is a one-man project . . . you don't want no destructive supervision). Try to avoid places with big rocks, roots, or hickory nuts. Stomp accurately. Try not to let the edges that will become the gunwales get crimped too bad. Don't worry about all those little heel dents. You don't want the boat to look like it was made by machinery.

Soon you will notice that the bottom of the boat is assuming a hogged shape and that the two stem heels (or toes) are lower than the place you are stomping. Don't worry about it. I read an article in *Messing About in Boats* that said that hogging of the keel is beneficial to performance. A long time ago when I was brazing these tin canoes together, completely oblivious to the fact that the zinc vapors from the galvanize were deadly, I used to cut a dart fore and aft along the keel to eliminate this hog that I thought was so ugly. Now I know better. It keeps the ends of the boat in the water so the waterline length is as long as possible all the time. You might have to look for a little hill to move the stomping operation to so the lay of the land won't interfere with the hogging of the bottom. As you pull the sides up with your hands and stomp a beautiful roundness into the turn of the bilge, you will notice that the two stems are beginning to tumble home back toward you sort of like an 1890s battleship. I used to try to trim the ends of the tin to avoid this back when I was letting imaginary aesthetics override my better judgment. That tumble-home increases waterline length and looks good to me. At the final stages of stomping, it is hard to keep from crimping the "sheer strake." Just try to keep from fatiguing the metal by crimping the same place over and over. It takes experience. Don't let yourself get frustrated and frantic . . . hell, man, tin is cheap.

Finishing Touches

Finally, you will have stomped and pulled a nice, lovely shape into the boat, but it will be too limber and dangerous along the gunwales. A piece of quarter-round screwed into the top "V" will cure that. No need for any 5200 (called "doo-get-around" in the trade) or even the ritual with the two kinds of flathead screws. Just use regular little sheet metal screws into predrilled holes. After you get through with that, spring for some of that black plastic pipe that used to be so common. Put it out in the yard in the hot sun until it gets soft enough to cut with a sharp linoleum knife. Lubricate the blade by dipping it into a jar of diesel fuel and rip that pipe, full length, all down one side. When the plastic starts pulling on the knife, dip it again. Don't slip and cut yourself. While the pipe is still hot, slip it over the quarter round and tin of the gunwales. I don't know what your experience is, but to me, that polyethylene pipe makes the best rub rail in the world, not just for tin canoes, but for any yacht tender. It is indestructible, cheap, and won't do any more damage to the paint (or gelcoat!) of a yacht than anything else. It is sort of eye-catching on a tin canoe. It is possible to fool folks into thinking you have something pretty cute if you paddle away real quick before they get a chance to examine it too closely.

Adjustment

This is a borderline vessel. The freeboard-beam ratio that I mentioned above might need to be re-stomped a little to suit the user. Fortunately, it can usually be done right there at pondside. There is one thing you ought to know, though. If your ass is much wider than ten inches (compressed) there ain't going to be a whole hell of a lot that you can do to bring the narrow range of the adjustment within the parameters of your big butt.

Performance

You are going to be in for a surprise. I know that a lot of you think that I have been teasing all along with all this tin canoe foolishness, but I'm serious. I have been in a lot of small, fast paddling boats, but there is nothing like a tin canoe. I don't know if it is the galvanized surface, the heel bumps on the bottom, the hog of the keel, or the shape that the sheet metal dictates, but it sure will fly. Even just paddling with your hands, the speed is astonishing. Weeds and lily pads don't seem to affect it at all. It just zips through the water. A double paddle helps keep it upright and makes it so that you can almost turn the thing a little, but you don't need it. The inability to turn the boat so it will go where you want it to is one drawback—along with the tippiness and the half inch of freeboard—but you know, ain't nothing perfect in this world.

When you hook a fish in one of those things, you have to work it a little differently. First, you have to be real careful not to get too excited or else you will either turn over or sink from not paying attention. The second thing is that, if there is any size to the fish at all, it is hard to tell who has whom. If the fish is anything but absolutely broadside to you, he (or she) will pull the boat off in a tack that is oblique to the line of the force and, in obeisance to the Newtonian Laws of Motion, the boat will continue like that until something stops it. You will probably pass right by the fish and go off in the wrong direction until the pull of the line finally stops the boat and reverses it. Then it will zip backward on the same line of travel, and either pass him again or cut him loose on the sharp tin stern (now stem) or hang the line on some weeds or a snag. If the fish is dead ahead when he gets hooked, he will just take you home with him. It is an adventure. The contest is much more even than when the fish is caught from a high-tech metal-flake monster bass boat. If you are trying to use a fly rod, I think the deal even favors the fish a little . . . if he could just figure out a way to take you home and eat you after he gets you in the water. Which . . . maybe an alligator . . .

One Last Thing

You don't want to litter the bottom of any body of water with carelessly sunk tin canoes. You need to tie a crab trap float to one of the stems with enough line so you can find it and swim the boat back to the bank to dump the water out. Doing that will test that ten-inch butt, too.

THE REYNOLDS

in which I learn the true meaning of life . . . when I am
young enough to make some good use of the knowledge

W<small>E HAD A</small> bunch of little boats when I was a boy, but the most important one was the Reynolds. I think I was about eight when I became captain of that worthy vessel. My family had always followed the laissez-faire method of child rearing and that old Reynolds made us all as free and wild as any civilized children could possibly be. My father was a writer so capable that he could make a living by just doing a little typing early in the morning before breakfast. Once he showed me, as an example, how easy it was. He wrote a story early in the morning and sent it off to a magazine in the first mail. The check, for fifteen hundred bucks— new car money in 1952—came two days later. I have never been able to do that, but because of the freedom of his life and the freedom of use of the Reynolds, I do know a thing or two about a thing or two.

Most of the time in warm weather (most of the time), we lived in a house on the beach about halfway between Carrabelle and East Point in the panhandle of Florida. It was a big ramshackledy old log house that was built around 1910 by one of the pioneer Florida rich men as a gift for his beloved and peculiar daughter. She never went to that house, not even one time. When we bought it in 1947, the carpenter's scraps and sawdust were still on the floors of all the rooms. There wasn't an electrical wire in the place. It had a railroad-style windmill well pump. At first, the only electrical thing was my father's old battery-powered Halicrafters radio, and the only machines were his typewriter, the car in the yard, and the outboard on the Reynolds.

That Reynolds was one of the pioneer aluminum boats, built by Reynolds Aluminum Company. I believe it was built before World War Two, because I am sure I remember it in 1946 when my father came back from the war and money couldn't buy any aluminum anything during the war. It was a pretty stylish old boat. The hull was shaped sort of like one of the "tri-hull" butt pounders of the sixties and seventies. It actually had a center "V" and two side convolutions of the bottom. The bow was round, with a big, useless foredeck and a streamlined, futuristic-looking cast aluminum cleat. The transom had the good tumblehome of the time (you can say what you want to about tumblehome, but the fact of the matter is, the shape makes a convexity to the rails in the stern that strengthens a small planing skiff). It had a red streak of lightning, factory painted down both sides, to make its intentions clear. The stern seat was big, U-shaped plywood and there was only one center seat. Between the center thwart and the stern was a peculiar thing. A spring-loaded, cast aluminum eye was welded into the bottom of the boat and stuck way up, most handily right in front of the man at the motor. Even now after some fifty years, my right hand still longs to grab that eye as I am standing at the tiller of any boat when it lurches wrong. Actually, I sort of miss the whole business.

That eye was part of a strange trailer arrangement. The Reynolds came with a humpbacked welded steel pipe trailer that straddled the boat with its wheels. There was a tongue that stuck into the spring-loaded eye of the boat and, by prying down on the hitch of the trailer, one (or two, if the motor was on it) could lift the old Reynolds right out of the water and hook it up to the car and drive off with it. It sounds like a wonderful idea, but there were several things that went wrong in our situation. First, we had to unhook the trailer from the car to hook up to the eye and then it was a struggle, with the heavy Reynolds hanging, to haul it uphill back to the trailer ball. Even when we got it hooked up, it didn't tow worth a damn with all that negative hitch weight. We always left the whole rig up in the sea oats and used the fool trailer only to launch the boat, and never hauled it over the road. Finally, the aluminum wheel hubs and the steel wheel bearings got together to finish off the whole trailer program; then we dragged the boat to the water. It was the children's boat and we did it eagerly.

The old Reynolds was only twelve feet long and built out of aluminum so thick that it might as well have been lead. It took us all to get it to the water, but then, after we clamped the motor on, like *Where the Wild Things Are*, the wild rumpus began. We were a hard-charging little crew. I was the oldest, so I was the boss. There were a variable number of my cousins, both boys and girls, some almost babies, and my two sisters and the girl (best friend of the oldest sister) who would wind up as my wife. Altogether, the whole bunch of children at the coasthouse averaged around seven or eight, and usually all of them wanted to go. As I said, we were not supervised by our parents at all—didn't even have to come home for meals, but if we did, there it was, if we could find it. We were even exempt from evening muster and often stayed out all night rampaging up and down the wild shore in that old Reynolds. When we ran out of gas, we just rowed and towed. Five little boogers on the towline are just about equivalent to five horsepower—better than that in the shallow water of the flats around here.

It would be easy to pass judgment on our parents and say that they were negligent. Of course, memory is selective, but I can't recall any time when we were in any more danger than if we had been "properly" supervised. Children who know that they are on their own are pretty cautious, and there were so many of us that the chance of a little one drowning, unnoticed, was pretty slim. Besides, around here, shallow water is more of a problem than deep. As they say, "On the flats, a man would have to dig a hole if he wanted to drown himself." We were always so busy going where we needed to go that there was no fighting or meanness. All we wanted to do was to facilitate the progress. Those grown folks going on with their own doings weren't negligent, not at all. You know, taking the whole summer off to go to the coast wasn't all that unusual in the Deep South back before megalomania and AC. Corn has made roasting ears before June, so the farming is over until fall. Besides, the sweat doesn't run into your eyes quite as bad down where the sea breeze blows. The grown people mostly stayed in the shade around the house but not us. We tried to wear out the water.

The whole Reynolds business took up several years and we all grew up while it happened. Little girls, the tops of their bathing suits hauled way down below their nipples (my skinny little wife-to-be, too) by the hard charging, had to change their ways. The intensity of our progress through the shallow water from one important destination to the other was such that the little ones usually wound up naked. There was one very persistent little fella. We tried to leave him at home because he was so slow, waddling along behind, but just about the time we would be getting in the boat, here he would come down the path from the house, hollering, "Wait the boat. . . . Wait the boat." When towing time came, he refused to be a non-participant and just ride in the boat. We dragged him while he held on to the painter, little naked body trailing along behind, diaper long gone, short legs working. We did that so much with that little boy that he had calluses on his hands before he was two, and because he always trailed along the same way on the towline, he was darker on one side than the other, kind of like a flounder. At least his bottom eye didn't drift around to the dark side. He still lives around here. Says his whole life has gone downhill since those days.

There was another little boy who had a black wool bathing suit that never seemed to get wet. He could swim around in it all day long and when he got out, his bathing suit was just as dry as anything. We all marveled at it and got him to let us try it on to see what it felt like. As the years went by, the moths ate bigger and bigger holes in his bathing suit and, when he took it off, he had a pattern of their work tanned onto his hide. He was a pusher.

I mean, when we towed the boat (which was most of the time) he pushed on the stern with one or two other little ones. Because of that, the moth hole patterns on his back side were darker than on the front. One time, he was pushing on the foot of the engine when it came unlatched and tilted down. He busted his lip something awful and didn't cry a single squawk even though he was only about five years old. He was a tough little booger, a neighbor kid, not of the family, so he had to go home to eat and sleep. I remember him trudging reluctantly off down the beach, all by himself when the time came. He is an electrical contractor in Tallahassee now, still has that scar on his lip from where he bit that chunk of aluminum out of the foot of that motor. He does not have that bathing suit anymore, though. I think Jacques Cousteau wound up with it.

As I said, these expeditions sometimes kept us away from the house for a long time. Though we always took, at my mother's insistence, five whole gallons of ice water in an old galvanized cooler with a ceramic liner (a heavy thing), the food usually ran short. The deformities of our civilized tastes disappeared in the face of plain starvation. We squatted like varmints on oyster bars, silently at work with our screwdrivers. The kid with the bathing suit loved the little oyster crabs and ate them raw . . . just chewed them up whole, sand and all. We had to open oysters for the little naked ones, but they didn't mind a little grit. We ate, immediately, every scallop we found—mantle, viscera, eyes, and all (to me, even now that my experience has broadened, there is no better snack). The whole time we were moving, we caught crabs and towed them along loose in the bottom of the boat, along with all the seashells that the little ones thought they had to take home (there is a modern "shell midden" where we dragged that old Reynolds up in the yard of that old house). When we got to a good stopping place, we would dip up some sea water in a foot tub, build a fire around it and boil all of those crabs. It was every man for himself when they got red. Sometimes, somebody nice like my wife-to-be would pick out some for the little naked ones, but usually, they did it for themselves. The little ones ate so much shell that their excrement looked about like that of coons or otters. One little four-toothed boy developed a strong liking for the contents of the crop and stomach of the crabs—called it "goody." If I had known then what I know now, I probably would have stopped him. At least it didn't hurt him in the long run, and who was I to decide what it takes to make the time that is the pinnacle of a man's whole life?

Those old wonderful wild and naked days seemed to last forever. It was as if I spent half my life with that old Reynolds, but the facts are the facts: What got the old boat was electrolysis and metal fatigue. It had wooden rub-rails and sheer clamps and three oak runners screwed into grooves to stiffen the bottom. After the rot and termites of the beach and gribbles of the sea had eaten those off, we patched the screw holes with some stuff called Celastic, which was a little piece of stiff cloth that, when wet with some special solvent, got very sticky and would stay on the aluminum pretty good. Though the bottom worked more in the chop and probably contributed to the fatal metal fatigue along the chines, the absence of the bottom runners was better for the boat than the replacement of them. One winter, my father and uncle put new mahogany runners and rails on the old boat. It sure looked good like that. The brass screws and stove bolts just gleamed beneath the varnish. They kept on gleaming all summer as the old Reynolds sacrificed itself to keep them shining. By the summer of fifty-five, most of the girls had pulled their bathing suits up, the babies were no longer naked, and the old Reynolds was leaking so bad that we couldn't keep up with it and we went on to other (actually better) boats. Some of us became responsible adults after that. Sometimes at a family gathering, two old executive types will exchange a certain look. One will say, "You remember that old Reynolds?" The other one will reply, "Did Elvis love his momma?"

THE REYNOLDS CREW DISCOVERS
ST. GEORGE ISLAND

and saves the day with a brave rescue

WE WERE CHILDREN of the flats. Around here, there are miles and miles of them. The shallow water covers sandy plains of grass that are almost continuous from Yucatán to the Keys. I read somewhere that the average decline of the bottom of the near-shore Gulf of Mexico is about a foot to the mile. The discovery of the wonderful diversity of the flats occupied us to the limit of our capacity. We tried our best to find out what lived in every hole (a never-ending quest—some of us are still at it after fifty years). When we found something interesting, we took it home for our folks to marvel at, and marvel they did. We dug enormous gulf quahogs as big as softballs. The hard and soft clams of the north Gulf of Mexico get much bigger than they do in the Atlantic, even down south on the East Coast of the peninsula. There has been some research on the quahogs that has established that they are the same species and can be mix-bred. I knew a man who made that his life's work. Though gulf hard clams get bigger sooner, they don't stay shut as well as Atlantic clams, so they gape and drool while they are out of the water and aren't at their best unless they are eaten before they do too much of that. This man was trying to breed the drooling out of them. I guess he finally did, but the whole project didn't pay off for him. Who wants to eat a quahog as big as a grapefruit besides my momma? A ghastly sight for the eyes of newcomers at our house.

We labored excitedly to dig huge, little-known, gulf soft-shell clams and angel wing clams as big as Coca-Cola bottles that lived in holes so deep that the excavations we left in the flats became landmarks. We dug stinking, stinging nemertean worms and all kinds of polychaetes. We discovered the remarkable commensal association of the terrible toadfish and the pistol shrimp, an association that has interested me all my life. They live together in a good-sized tunnel cut through the roots of the turtle grass (*Diplanthera* usually). When the tide is out, it is possible to root around and dig them out. The toadfish acts like he doesn't care— he knows what he'll do to you if you mess with him—but the little shrimp hides so adroitly in the muddy water that he is hard to find. With that toadfish looking at you like that, it is hard to feel around adequately. My slapdash experiments have shown that though toadfish are not afraid of anything, they do not eat pistol shrimp (which is a good shrimp raw, kinda small for cooking). A regular *pinead* shrimp is a goner as soon as the toadfish sees him, even if he has to spit out some half-swallowed other morsel to make room. But you can starve a toadfish down to where he is visibly hollow-bellied, and he won't make a pass at even a declawed pistol shrimp. I don't think I have it completely figured out, but I believe that, unlikely as it might seem, the pistol shrimp is the boss of the hole. It might be that the toadfish looks at a disarmed shrimp with caution (can't tell—might have that pistol in his pocket). The relationship might be of mutual benefit. The hole undoubtedly allows toadfish to live higher on the flats where they would dry out at low tide if they didn't have the water in the shrimp hole, and the terrible toadfish might provide some protection for the shrimp, but I am not so sure that the shrimp can't take care of himself. There is no question that it is the shrimp who makes the hole. They can do it without the help of any toadfish and, indeed, there are plenty of fishless shrimp holes on the flats (and shrimp-hole-less toadfish farther out), which leads me to believe that the relationship between the two denizens is completely one-sided. The shrimp is just the host of the terrible toadfish. I'll tell you this for your own good. A big toadfish is a dangerous thing. Not only will they fin you with poisonous spines, they will bite the fool out of you. They are sort of diabolical with it. You don't have to stick your finger or toe in their mouths for them, they'll reach over there and grab you. It is hard to get loose, too. We soon learned not to let toadfish have free run of the bilgewater of the Reynolds like the crabs. A crab sort of makes his intentions known and is hard to ignore, but a toadfish will lurk around and get you when you ain't paying attention.

We chased stingarees and hemmed flounders up in shallow pools. We marveled at the ferocity of the soft crab's husband and took her away from him anyway. We squatted in the short sea grass and fed the big burrowing anemones to see what they liked. Burrowing anemones live attached to the bottom of a hole they excavate in the sandy bottom of the flats. When the tide is out, they retract and deflate their tentacles so that they are flush with the surface and don't look like much of anything. When they are covered by water, they extend the tentacles and look like a sea anemone. Though they are tolerant of inspection, if you bother them too much, they will retract way down into their holes. They are eager feeders on most any kind of fresh meat, alive or dead, and can hold on to and ingest surprisingly large fish, crabs, and worms. Their favorite food is a shucked oyster. They get so excited when they detect the juice that you think they might turn loose and come hopping out of their hole.

We swam under the floating grass and found sea horses by listening to the snap they made when they ate some tiny creature. We made pools where we kept them with the Sargasso fish, tiny puff fish, and other peculiar things that we caught. Sea horses mostly eat tiny crustaceans that crawl around on the stems of sea grass. They are slow and deliberate-acting little things and it is hard to imagine how they could possibly catch anything. They have a neat trick, though. When they see an amphipod or tiny shrimp, they lean over in that direction and slowly stick their nose as close to the prey as they can without scaring him off. When they are close enough, they tense up their cheeks and with a little pop noise, open their tiny mouths and the crustacean vanishes from the grass . . . sucked in so fast, it is hard to see exactly how it works.

The Yucatán Current, a major component of the Gulf Stream, makes a loop far to the north in the Gulf of Mexico. All sorts of strange plants and creatures wash up on the beach around here, including Sargasso weed with its unusual inhabitants. Looking carefully while swimming along in a patch of floating weeds is a fascinating thing for young children who are interested in strange creatures (and all children are before TV and puberty numbs their skulls). There are few stranger-looking things than a Sargasso fish, except maybe for puff fish. There are two kinds of puff fish around here, the spiny kind and the smooth kind. Both of them are easy to catch and good to eat if they are big enough. You just skin them, cut off the head, and eat the backbone part. The soft bones are child safe. Don't eat the liver, and never put one of the spiny kind in your bathing suit pocket.

We were delighted when we discovered a tiny, cunning octopus who holds himself between two sunray Venus clam shells with his strong little arms. The octopi are just about the size of a scallop's abductor muscle and have very short arms. At night, they forage around in the grass and catch little crabs and such, but during the day, they close themselves up in a pair of often mismatched clam shells. They hold on to one side with four arms and grab the other shell with the other four and hold it closed just like a new abductor muscle. They have a pretty good grip, too, but if you do pry the two shells apart, they'll give a little squirt of ink and disappear so completely that six sharp-eyed children can't find them. Sometimes they'll stay in a gastropod shell and hold something like a sand dollar or a broken piece of shell over the hole sort of like an operculum. If you pull that loose, sometimes they'll squirt and hide, but sometimes they will retreat way back inside the volutes of the shell. If you root around down in there with your finger, the miniature octopus will bite a cute little piece of meat out of you. Because of experiences such as that, there were four-year-old children in our crew who knew more of the animals of the flats than most of the graduate students at the FSU marine lab did when I was there in the late sixties.

Sometimes, but not often, we would see another boat. Usually, it was a beach seiner, which was a fascinating thing to us children. This species of commercial fishing has been extinct in the gulf since about 1954 or so. The fishermen cruised up and down the coast in shallow draft inboard motor boats about thirty-five or forty feet long. Even as late as this, some of those boats were old converted sailboats called luggers. (Down near the delta they carried the very fast and weatherly but reputedly dangerous French style dipping-lug rig, but up here, they were rigged as gaff schooners. They were well built out of good stuff and there are still a few around; one down in Apalachicola right now was built in 1877.) The net was carried in two big rowing skiffs that were towed along behind. When a school of mullet was sighted, the big boat was anchored well offshore and the skiffs were rowed ashore, one up the beach of the fish, the other down. They ran out the big, heavy, tarred cotton seine over the stern. When the strike was complete, all the men (at least six, sometimes eight) grabbed the net and, running down the beach toward each other, drew the two ends together, completely encircled the fish. Then, pulling as hard as they could, leaning way back, bare heels digging deep, they drew the net to the beach by both ends. As they pulled, they backed down the beach with the longshore current leaving the already pulled in part of the net strung out in the shallow water behind them.

Eventually, they would have a good-sized bag full of frantic fish, which they would haul as close in as possible. Then they would empty as many of the fish out with a dip net and their hands as they could, throwing the catch into a big box in the stern of each skiff. Many of the fish would jump out, especially the wonderfully intelligent and agile mullet, the prize of the haul. Crabs and other "trash" were either thrown out or left alone until later. As they lightened the net, they pulled more of it in. Sometimes they would catch so many fish (mostly mullet, but a few speckled trout, redfish, flounder, and sometimes Spanish mackerel) that the boxes would fill up, then they just threw the fish in the bottom of the boats. Though the men were skilled at what they were doing, sometimes they would get finned by a catfish or a stingaree. At that I must explain something to you. Only ignorant people call stingarees "stingrays," possums "opossums," and coons "raccoons."

These beach seiners were tough, I tell you. They just flung the fish off and kept on as if it hadn't happened. I have been finned by those things myself, and it is a hard injury to ignore. Sometimes there would be a shark in the net fixing to bite out. As soon as they saw him, one of the men would wade out into the boiling mass of cooped-up fish with the gaff. We children would stand and marvel at the fury as the man gaffed the shark, picked the head of the violently thrashing fish up as high as possible, and dragged him out of the net.

We were shy of these wonderful people, but it was hard to keep the little ones aloof from such as that. One time, before we knew what had happened, the littlest one had clapped onto the net and was helping haul. The men tried their best not to step on him and we tried our best to dislodge him from the meshes without getting in the way, but he hung on until the end. As they left, I, as the oldest, waded out to apologize, but I was too late. As powerful strokes of the oars took the loaded net skiff out through the low surf, I heard the only words from those men. One said, "You know, that little naked booger pulled pretty good to be so gaptoothed." The next time we saw that same boat, the men silently made room and motioned us up. We all clapped on . . . silently. It was easy to tell the difference in the progress of the project, too. After that, there was a noticeable difference in the level of noise around our boat. We admired the silence of those men. To this day, I do not allow hollering on board of my boats. My wife and I can, wordlessly, beat our thirty-foot sailboat out of most any narrow little place right into a dead wrong wind. Of course, I raised her from a child.

After the silent men had loaded up and gone, the beach would be littered with the rejects from the net. We, after a glance to make sure that we were finally alone, fell on these creatures, things too fast for us to catch on the flats. We examined the marvelous cutlass fishes with their terrible teeth. We found out the hard way about the shocking stargazer and the electric ray. We felt the sharp ventral ridge of the pogies (menhaden). We examined the Maurice Sendak faces of lizard fish (we called them "sharp-nosed boogers," a better name) and the delightful cowfish with only his fins and lips outside the fused scales that formed his triangular cross-sectioned shell. We took home the first one of those that we found and my momma called him a "trunkfish" and taught us to cook him by rolling him around in the fire, West Indian fashion. As an example of simple cooking paying off, it is hard to beat a trunkfish rolled in a pine straw fire until the steam comes out around his tail.

Not only were we biologists, ecologists, and gourmets, but archaeologists and paleontologists, too. It didn't take us long to find the tailings from where the shell middens of the other wild people of this place were being cut out by the waves as the sea continued its rise across the flats from the far-off shore of the Pleistocene. We found the broken pieces of pottery that had been discarded long ago with the shells of the same oysters, clams, and conchs that had become so familiar to us. We marveled at how many those people must have eaten to make such a pile of shells. We especially loved the thin pieces of pottery that had been decorated in antiquity by some little wild girl by digging in the soft clay with her little fingernail, repeatedly, in an intricate pattern. We could see in the long-ago print just exactly how the clay and her fingernail had been—how soft the clay and how long, how big, how thick her fingernail. We would look among us for someone who had a perfect match and vow to make us just such a pot one day.

In the bottoms of the dark creeks, we found the black bones of long-gone animals—the huge molars of mastodons and mammoths, the knuckles of manatees, the patterned shell bones of giant turtles, the jigsaw-puzzle pieces of the shells of armadillos. Half the things we brought home in the bottom of the old Reynolds were unidentifiable by the folks at the house, and even now one of us will come across a picture in a book somewhere and call a conference. We'll straggle in to have a look and exclaim, "Oh, that's what that was!" We found a dugout canoe, partially embedded in the silt of the bottom of a pool in one of the little spring-fed creeks where we went many days in a futile attempt to hem in mullet. We tried to dig it out and raise it, but it was too big and slippery for us. Years later, one of us tried to interest an anthropologist at FSU in that canoe, but he never got around to making the trip way back in there. I did, though, not long ago, and though the water was too high and dark to get a look, I could feel it with my feet. I think I'll let it stay there.

One day, while we were up in that same wonderful little creek catching crabs, we saw a yellow biplane with a good-sounding engine. Now I know it for an old Stearman, like so many that were sold off as surplus after the war and were flown to death dusting DDT onto tobacco fields. We watched it follow the same shore that was becoming so familiar to us by then; then it banked and flew out to sea and, as we watched, began to fly along the shore of a distant island that we had barely noticed in our pre-occupation with the flats. Our attention was focused. We began to make plans.

We made a special arrangement with my mother to help us get ready to go to the island—extra gas, extra water, some gro-ceries. Some of us thought about trying to get her to help us side-track the little naked ones, but we knew it was no use—they had seen the airplane and heard the plans being made. Early the next morning, we set off. It was kind of strange to run the old outboard motor for so long. It seemed to me that we ran over the slick calm water for a mighty long time before the island started getting any closer, but after a while, we could see details of the beach—sea oats, dunes, clear little waves curling along the shore. When I shut off the engine and we slid up, it was certainly a different kind of place. We all hopped out onto the strange new land, St. George Island.

We became obsessed with that place. The flats were forgotten. We ran amok. Our parents had to make daily trips to town for gas after that. It is easy to think that they went on with their daily doings without giving us a thought, but I know the binoculars ("knobblers" in the family language from some long-grown-up child's pronunciation) were well focused when the time came for the afternoon sea breeze to bring us back in.

St. George Island at that time was not only completely uninhabited, but was almost unvisited. Someone had some cows over there and we were wary of them, but eagerly used their cow-plops for fuel to cook our crabs because, on our end, there were no trees to make the pine straw and pine cones that we usually piled around our foot tub. We discovered many new things over there, but we were particularly excited by relics of the Army that were everywhere. During WWII, St. George Island was used as a practice beachhead by trainees from Camp Gordon Johnston, which stretched along the coast from where Lanark is now, nearly to Ochlocknee Bay.

Now St. George Island is the most expensive real estate in Franklin County and overrun with all-terrain vehicles, Jet Skis, and party animals, but in the early fifties, when we were rampaging over there, about the only signs of humanity were rusty old bombs, nose down in the sand among the cow plops. We found a tiny island covered with big bullets (fifty-caliber Browning machine gun, we would later learn). The vets told us that the pilots probably used that island as a target for strafing with aircraft. We loaded the old Reynolds up with those artifacts. (All that brass probably contributed to the eventual electrolytic destruction of the old boat. Just the slightest swipe of brass or copper on aluminum will take its toll.) One day, after we had rampaged up the bayside shore and picked up all the bullets we needed, we noticed that the sky was getting dark and dangerous-looking. We were almost to the place where the trees and high dunes started, so we decided to hurry on down there to take shelter. We had had a lot of experience with the swift, violent thunderstorms of the Gulf of Mexico, and by then had established a quick little ritual.

Those storms are almost an everyday occurrence during the summertime and are caused by the difference in temperature of the land and the shallow water, both hot as hell. Usually, during the day, the land gets much hotter than the hot water and a sea breeze is drawn in by the updraft convection over the land. As this humid air from the sea rises, each molecule of water vapor gives up the heat energy that excited it into evaporating in the first place. Soon the heat released by all those little molecules as they condense causes a cumulus cloud that towers from the height of first condensation all the way to the stratosphere (the height above which water vapor cannot rise without condensing, because the air is so rare and cold) and sometimes from horizon to horizon. After dark, the land cools quickly and then it is the hot water that causes the convection upward. The result is a land breeze and thunderstorms that build over the water until the sun comes up in the morning. Either way, clouds that grow into the upper levels of the troposphere often get blown in unpredictable directions, so Gulf Coast seagoing people soon learn to keep a weather eye out. The summer storms of the gulf come up quick and blow hard. In five minutes, the shallow inshore gulf can be transformed from a fiercely hot dead calm into such a sea that no boat can maintain planing speed and even seagoing tugs have to head up for a while. Often, the lightning is continuously visible . . . a bad situation to be in, either at sea or such a lightning bait place as St. George Island.

When we saw a storm coming, we ran for the beach and quickly took the engine off and turned the boat upside down, stern to the wind with the foredeck propped up on the engine and water jug. The little ones would hide under the boat and us big ones would take shelter in the dunes as best we could unless there was lightning, then it was a tight little huddle with us all under the Faraday's cage of aluminum. Though the wind sometimes got up enough to hammer the boat pretty good, it was never snatched loose from the strong hands of the little ones. After the storm had passed and we resumed our navigation, there would be a strange track left on the beach from where the children under the boat had swiveled the transom around to keep it to windward as the storm swept by.

This time, when we arrived at the place where we planned to turn the boat over, we found another boat—the first we had seen on St. George Island. We quickly unloaded and turned the old Reynolds upside down. We noticed that there were some people, too. We could see them waving at us from up the beach, where they were ignorantly standing under some trees trying to bait up a little lightning. We could tell that the mosquitoes were eating them up. We didn't have time to exchange greetings before the blow brought the stinging sand and drove them back to the trees. When the rain came, though it stung us outside ones, too, it was better than the dry sand. Immediately, those people's boat began to drag its anchor. If it hadn't been for quick work by my oldest sister and my wife-to-be in the strong SW wind, it would have been gone down the bay. They squatted in the driving rain and held the little iron-lump-style Navy anchor down in the hard sand until the blow was over. It was lucky for those people that there was no lightning, because my wife-to-be did not like it and does not to this day, and would have quickly abandoned the project.

Those summer storms usually pass just as quickly as they come up, and pretty soon the mosquitoes were eating us all up again. We children put the Reynolds back in and began to load her up. I guess those people thought that we were getting ready to leave them because they came running. They turned out to be two couples of college students from FSU. Their boat was out of fix and they were stranded, had been all day long. The food was eaten, the drinks were drunk and the shade was scarce and they were glad to see us. Since the Reynolds was too little to take all of us to the mainland, we agreed to tow them. Because of the direction of the wind, I decided to take them directly home to our house instead of where they wanted to go. At first, it was not too bad. Even though the sea was still up pretty good from the leftovers of the thunderstorm, it was in a fair direction and their big, heavy, inboard boat, propeller dragging, came along noticeably on the towline.

The boat was a Correct Craft, plywood, inboard runabout about eighteen feet long. We saw it all the time after the initial rescue. It turned out that one of the girls of that crew had a summer house about a mile down the beach east of us and attracted the male owner of the Correct Craft quite often. As is frequently the case with people who have boats like that, the boat had been left wallowing in the waves at the water's edge while the cavorting was going on. The tide went out and this fellow thought that the enormous horsepower of the flathead Ford V-8 would shake the boat loose from the sand. What actually happened was that the sand shook that engine loose from its horsepower.

Before it got dark, the wind shifted more to the northwest and that slowed us down. We discovered that their boat was half full of water and we had to stop and give them something to bail with and tell them to center the rudder so our little engine could make a little better progress. After dark came, the usual backward wind sprang up from the land and it was slow going for real. Finally, we had to head directly for Porter Bar to make any headway toward the mainland at all. When the gas gave out, we were in our old stomping grounds, though still some few miles downwind of the house. Sleepy children piled out onto the flats and took up the towline in the dark as if they had been doing it all their lives. It was slow progress, too. Not only was that other boat heavy, we had to keep out where it was deep enough for the propeller and rudder and go slow so we could drag our feet for stingarees.

Except for lightning storms, stingarees are the most dangerous natural thing at the coast around here. There are more people waiting in the emergency rooms of Florida because of stingarees than from injuries inflicted by all other natural hazards combined. Only fools wade in water where they can't see the bottom without shuffling their feet for stingarees. If you slide your feet, you will touch the ray and scare him away before you can step on him. If you step on a stingaree, he will instantly arch his tail and slide the lubricated spine that is loosely attached at the base of his tail into your ankle. The spines of stingarees and catfish are encapsulated by a slimy membrane of poisonous stuff (not usually infectious in stingarees, but very much so in catfish, especially freshwater catfish). Not only are those spines poisonous, but they are serrated— barbed in a most exquisite way. Only flesh knows flesh. A stingaree spine will stay with you like nothing else I ever saw. If they stay in you, you are in trouble. Some say that it is possible to grab the end with a pair of pliers and sort of unscrew the spine so that the barbs won't take so much meat as it is pulled out, but the idea never appealed to me all that much. I think they must be cut out and they hold on until the last barb. A lot of the folks down here have some bad-looking scars where the skin of a long, homemade incision didn't heal back straight—kind of like a crossbuttoned shirt. When I got hit while I was doing a bottom job on my sailboat on the flats of Dog Island, my momma, then in her dotage, said that the best thing to do was to soak your foot in the hottest water you can stand while you drink all the whiskey in the house, and it worked so good that I was able to ignore the injury and go back and finish the job (turned out kind of sloppy). It was only after the thing had healed and I began to walk funny that I finally went to the doctor to find the spine embedded in the tendons of my ankle. My mother always carried a nine-inch stingaree spine in her pocketbook. She said that it was for self-defense, but I know that it was to impress little boys with.

More to the point, believe it or not, one of those FSU women declined to participate in the towing work, and we had to haul her, too, like Cleopatra on her barge. I am wary of women like that and try to stay clear of them. We delivered those people into the company of my father, who introduced them to the martini. That little glass was a fixture of our house all through the fifties. It would be easy to think that our freedom was somehow connected, but it wasn't. Though the daily martini party started early and lasted late, there were quite a few adults, my mother included, who only rarely joined in. They fished and fooled around in the other boats and cooked and swept sand out of the house. When we came home for gas or something, there were usually people we had never seen before sitting around on the porch, laughing and poking at the olive in their martinis. Another day, on that porch, I saw a sunburned young woman (might have been Cleopatra) peel a slice of skin off herself that went much farther down inside her clothes than I would have expected. I wanted to hang around to see if it would have the nipple on it like the eye on the shed skin of a snake, but the children were already loading up and ready.

ANOTHER REYNOLDS RESCUE

*in which I escape formal education
but become educated nevertheless*

ONE TIME, WE went in the Reynolds in company with another boat to St. George Island with the whole coasthouse crew, not just the children, but the martini party from the porch, too. What had happened was that the constituents of the porch crew had gradually gotten younger and younger as the Reynolds crew got older and older. Some of us graduated to the porch as puberty infected us, and that accounts for a little of the change, but the main thing was that my father's books were selling very well and some of the "young adults" they were aimed at were groupy-ing around and they were so young that they got tired of sitting on the porch listening to the scintillating conversation. The books were adventurous and attracted adventurous fans, and I guess they saw us children out there passing by in the old Reynolds and, kind of like a dog looking at a car he wants to chase and then back at the porch he is supposed to stay on, they just kind of drifted out the screen door.

I think I was fifteen the summer the Reynolds saved all those people. The reason I remember my age was because that was the year I skipped the ninth grade. I didn't skip it because I was so smart that the school put me up a grade—well, that ain't exactly accurate. I skipped it because I was so smart that I put *myself* up a grade. I hope the statute of limitations has run out on things like this, because I have to admit something to you. I never was all that big on school (can you tell?) and I was a real hooky artist. Not only did I skip whole days at school, I was so slick that there were some classes I never attended when I was in attendance— things like English and PE, a lot of what they now call "Social Studies," and all of Health. "Brush your teeth after every meal." That's horseshit. Other animals don't brush their teeth, and unless they have been inbred-for-cute too much, they don't have any trouble with them. I think that scum protects the teeth from decay. After my father ran away to California about 1957, he got him a new wife and she used to brush the teeth of her standard poodle with an electric toothbrush. Jesus, the poor dog shivered like she was freezing to death the whole time—the poor animal did the same thing when they took her to get bred. The offspring were supposed to be worth a thousand bucks apiece. Too bad it didn't work, and then her teeth fell out, too.

So, my education wound up sort of spotty. I never did find out the importance of why saliva changes sugars to starches and starches to sugars and I don't know the names of all the presidents of the United States or the capital cities of each and every one of the states, nor am I all that knowledgeable about the intricacies of old English royalty. I do know about the divorcée Wallis Simpson, though. I slept at the Indiantown Inn, where she had worked as a waitress—might have slept in the same bed. Skipping school really didn't do me much damage in the long run . . . so far. I know a thing or two about a thing or two and did back when I was fifteen years old, too.

There was this girl that was hanging around the coasthouse then. She was, I guess, about twenty-two years old. She was one of the instigators of the "leave the porch" movement and I liked her fine. Back then, I was in the middle of my stingaree spine collection. I had a quart gin bottle (guess where it came from) almost full of stingaree spines. At first I was sticking the poor things with a regular, barbless, flounder gig. I didn't want to kill the creature, I just wanted to pull his (or her . . . female stingarees get much bigger than males) spine off with my old rusty water-pump pliers and put it in my gin bottle. Too bad there wasn't any gin left in there, because it stank like the dickens when I unscrewed the cap. By the time of this rescue, I was trying to get the biggest of those marvelous spines I could, and St. George had (and still has) some of the biggest stingarees I have ever seen anywhere. A flounder gig won't hold a ray as big as the shadow of a Volkswagen, though, so I laboriously filed myself a little harpoon head out of an all-steel oyster knife and I stuck the flounder gig into a little hole I had drilled (burnt up and broke about thirty-four of my father's drill bits) in it. When I stuck a stingaree, the head would go all the way through the wing and come off the gig, turn sideways, and toggle to him (her) with fifty feet of ⅜-inch Manila line. She would have to come on in then. Boy, I had some big stingaree spines in my bottle by the time of this particular rescue.

Before I saved all those people, I had to save myself from this girl. The peculiarities of my education and social life had left me unprepared for the rigors of puberty. The few times I attended school, I was sort of a social outcast. I wasn't a wretch like these modern killer-jerks or anything. I wasn't even unhappy with my status. I just didn't fit in. My clothes were a good example. All the other boys my age wore tight blue jeans hauled down as low as possible to the pubic bone and they all had a waxed, flattop hairdo, mowed off plumb bald in the middle of the top. Me, I wore my father's old passed-down khaki pants. They were too big, so I hauled them up high and cinched them up tight (my hairdo was what could best be called "shaggy bristles"). Those pants and the Weldwood glue and model airplane cement (Ambroid) that I dribbled and wiped on my clothes sort of kept the girls off me. Which was a good thing, because, starting about the time of this incident, I have had a lot of trouble with them.

I had better tell you why I skipped the whole ninth grade (I'll tell you how later), and then I'll get back to how the old valiant Reynolds rescued all those people from St. George Island. I already knew all the science and algebra because of my mother and father, who both knew how to cut right straight to the facts of the matter, and I just couldn't see anything else they had up there at the school that would be of any use to me. Which, you know, I don't believe they have improved education all that much since then. I am going to step out on a limb here; school ain't worth a flip.

So what happened over there on St. George Island was that this twenty-two-year-old woman decided that she needed to reveal to me the true depth of my ignorance, which was not so deep as she imagined. During my year off from school, I had read the complete *Memoirs of Casanova*, all fifty pounds' worth, and that'll educate a person beyond what is normally expected.

"Have you ever kissed a girl?" was how it started.

"Yeah, I kissed my sisters on the cheek when they were sweet little babies," was my reply.

"No," she said, "I mean, have you ever kissed a girl, not related to you, on the lips?"

"Nope, never wanted to do that, seems kind of nasty to me . . . you know, kind of like how chickens copulate."

"Well, you are mistaken," she stated assertively (she was in college studying to be a schoolteacher). "It's not nasty and the chickens don't think so, either, and I am going to show you."

Fortunately I was able to outrun her easily . . . didn't even have to drop my gin bottle or my harpoon.

All this carrying on sort of kept us from keeping a weather eye out. All of us children would have instantly noticed, if we had been on our own, but we were too distracted by the complications of the new social situation. The first hint we socializing fools had was when the sun got cut off and the sand began to blow into the pimento cheese sandwiches and the White Boat began to drag anchor.

I guess I'll have to tell you about that boat. I think it might have been the first fiberglass runabout ever made. My father loved a modern gadget more than anybody I ever knew, and I believe he might have had an interest in the company. Anyway, it was a Winner fifteen-foot fiberglass boat, built, I believe, in 1953. It was as stark white as anything I have ever seen. You could hardly look at it in the bright sun. It was also extremely heavy . . . about half an inch thick. The Reynolds would run rings around it with a seven and a half, and it had a thirty. It was a good sea-boat, though, and very dry. The designer went to the max with the new medium and put a bow on there that couldn't be done with anything other than bent-to-broke strip planking. It had a hollow to the forefoot like the inside of a spoon, and cheeks like Shirley Temple. Then it flared, uselessly, out to the foredeck (blue—thank goodness) like the bow of an aircraft carrier. It had a plastic windshield on it at first, but that useless thing soon disappeared along with the silly steering wheel and all those ridiculous cables and controls, including the starter switch. You know, if you have to have all that in a fifteen-foot skiff, you are overloading your lifestyle with unreliability. As soon as my father ran off to California to write for the movies and TV (he wrote a lot of the Perry Masons), we cleaned up that old White Boat and I eventually put an old war surplus storm boat motor on it and, for the first time, got that old, heavy tub up on a sure-enough plane.

I hate to keep interrupting this story, but the damn thing is already ruined and I need to explain the evolution of the ways to start an outboard motor so you'll understand some of the frustration to come. Old Ole Evinrude might have been the man who invented the cursed things, and the first one was started by grabbing a little knob sticking out of the flywheel on top of the motor and giving it a spin. The damned thing has gone downhill ever since: Next, they put a little groove in the top of the flywheel to wrap a rope around (indeed, called "rope wrapper" in the family lexicon). You pulled the rope to spin the flywheel. The trouble with that is—after the engine is started and demanding attention to keep running—what the hell do you do with the rope, loose it, throw it down in the bilgewater? Next came the "recoil starter," which had a little spring-loaded spool that recoiled the rope after you pulled. The trouble with that is the damned things hardly ever work right for very long. It is very common to see a lawn mower or a chain saw with the starter rope hanging out like the tongue of a hot dog. When in a fit of frustration you snatch the rope completely out of the Weed Eater, you just have to stop eating weeds, but when the recoil starter messes up ten miles out on the flats—well, there you are. The next diabolical "improvement" was electric starting. I won't explain all that. I'll just tell you my opinion. I do not trust machinery of any kind. I never go out in a boat that cannot be propelled some other way. I'll be damned if I'll undignify myself by sitting helplessly out there in the hot sun dialing 911 on a cellular phone. I would rather row thirty miles, and indeed I have.

But on the day of the storm when I outran the schoolteacher, that White Boat with both electric and recoil starters was dragging anchor rapidly out into the deep water of the pass. When my father and I finally caught the damn thing with the Reynolds, it was way out into the pass and the wind was blowing for real. He got off onto the White Boat and tried to start it with the key, but the battery was dead from a short in the bilge pump, so he had to climb back in the stern to open the door in the shroud of the engine and reveal the pull rope. Then the remote-controlled choke rig way up there in the dashboard wouldn't let him choke the thing right, and he pulled and pulled until he finally snatched the rope out of the recoil starter. By then, it was way too rough to hang over the transom and do all that mechanicking, so I took him in tow—finally. It was a sure-enough slow, crooked trip back to the little forlorn-looking crowd standing on the east-end point of the island in the driving rain.

And it kept on getting rougher all the time. If it had been these days, the little artificial German on the weather radio would have told us that this wasn't just another thunderstorm, but a major meteorological event. If it had developed a little farther down by Yucatán, it would have made a hurricane and, as it was, it stormed for two days. When we finally got loaded up to head back, it was a borderline situation, and if St. George hadn't been so inhospitable a place to spend two days on, we would not have risked it. But we knew we were looking at a dismal prospect, so we decided to make a try. The wind was about straight out of the west—right down the bay—and we had to crab up into it to make any headway toward the mainland. It was far too rough to go directly because the shallow bay was making a breaker out of each of those waves, and if we let the bow fall off too much, we couldn't bail fast enough—even though we had plenty of eager people and containers (bailing a boat for five hours is a good way to wash pimento cheese out of a bowl). Most of the people were huddling down in the White Boat. All you could see of them was the water they were throwing over the side. My mother and Bruzwully and I were the only ones in the Reynolds. I was running the engine and dodging the towline made up to the trailer eye, and which was trying to gnaw my ears off that day. My father and the rest of the crew finally got the White Boat trimmed to tow without yawing, but it was still slow going. We needed more line so we could get adjusted to the wavelength, but we didn't have it, and besides, by the time we got out there and under way, it was too rough to fool with any changes. It was a good thing that we had sense enough to get the gas cans out of the White Boat before we left, because there certainly would be no handing over of anything from then on, and the engine of the Reynolds burned a lot of gas that day.

That Reynolds engine was an Evinrude eighteen. Back in those days, Evinrude made two models out of the same engine. An eighteen was also a twenty-five, like a nine point nine is a fifteen now. They did that for years. As far as I could tell, there was not any difference in the two engines at all except for the bore of the carburetor—and the price. That's another example of what happens to people who spend too much time in school. They get so indoctrinated into accepting bullshit that they'll buy into a scam like that.

You know, the memory of really hard times sort of misses getting properly embedded in the brain. I don't remember much of that trip. I remember that the rain was cold and the spray was warm and that is about all. I guess I sat back there and tried to head up into the biggest of the waves while Momma and Bruzwully bailed and swapped gas tanks all day long. I just forgot about the White Boat trying to snatch us into a broach all the time. It was a long, miserable trip, though. You'll just have to take my word for it.

Years later I had another long miserable trip that I don't remember much about. My wife and I sailed straight across the Gulf from Dog Island to Pass-a-Grille down around Tampa Bay in our old raggedy Morgan thirty. I would have made another plan when it started breezing up that time, but my son and his new wife were waiting for us there on his sailboat and expecting us to show up. I didn't want to worry him when it started storming, so we beat right dead into it for what seemed like three or four days. I couldn't open the companionway but just a little crack and didn't dare quit the lookout for fear of getting run over in the poor visibility, so I stayed up there in the cockpit, wrapped up in the sail cover, and tried to duck the solid green water coming over the bow. I think that's the only time I ever looked *up* at a spotted porpoise. The only sail I could carry was just the reefed-to-nothing main, and it wasn't doing anything. My little thirty-year-old, twelve-horse Volvo was all that was accomplishing anything at all. That and my wife down there with the radio direction finder and the saltines with her feet jammed against one side of the dinette and her back against the other. All I remember of the trip was watching the crack in the companionway for her to pass me another saltine.

So the heroic rescuers and the shivering rescued finally waded ashore at the coasthouse. Most of them—those who could get a car to start—headed on back to high ground, but some of us had to stay to try to take care of the Reynolds and the White Boat, which had to ride at anchor through the rest of the storm. My father, gallantly, offered to let my twenty-two-year-old pursuer take his Porsche (356A Speedster just like James Dean killed himself with); when the Porsche wouldn't start, she was stuck with us remnants to wait the storm. Me and Bruzwully and some other children played Monopoly with her when we weren't bailing the boats. Except for a little hiding of money, there was no hanky-panky. I think she might have learned her lesson.

I almost forgot that I was going to tell you *how* I skipped the ninth grade. I just never went on the first day. I had a special driver's license since I was fourteen and drove the car that hauled all the other children. When I finished dropping them off at their schools, I just kept on driving. It was a very educational year. When the time came to go to high school, I just went to the tenth grade. They didn't find out about it until I was ready to graduate out of the twelfth. They were very perplexed about what to put into my permanent record. Didn't bother me a bit. I enlisted in the Navy, where I was perfectly safe from twenty-two-year-old girls.

A FEW RECIPES OF
THE REYNOLDS CREW

in which I begin a lifetime as a gourmet

B ACK IN THE good old days (which are still around for some)
my mother sort of looked after us to keep us from the ex-
tremities of bowel stress. We took various things with us from the
house to help out with the hunting and gathering. Usually we had
baked potatoes, apples, bananas, and sometimes those old staples
of skiffboat people all over: Vienna sausages and sardines. We
finally quit taking saltine crackers because of all the mishaps, but
we often had a hot watermelon rolling around in the bottom of
the boat with the stomped-on baked potatoes and apples. We
never brought anything back and we never got tired of the same
old thing.

THE REYNOLDS RECIPES

Oysters

Oysters are good. You can't eat lunch in a more natural way than squatting on an oyster bar until you get through. Now that they are apt to kill you or leave you with a disabled liver because of the nastiness of our civilization and the nature of their feeding, it is wise not to eat them raw, but that is how they are best. Though they might appear to some to be sort of amorphous, they are regular pelecypods with the same symmetry. . . . Not only do they have right and left, front and rear, they, like scallops, have top and bottom. Any child can quickly learn how they lie in the hand. A hungry, innocent child goes straight for the umbones and gnaws and wiggles with the screwdriver until the shells are separated at the hinge. I still do it that way. The oyster in the shell is (after scraping the abductor muscle free of the bottom shell) sucked up and, depending on the size, chewed or swallowed whole. After we had marauded our way west on St. George to where the trees began, we began to find some very big single oysters just lying around on the bottom. Some of them were as big as the bottom of a tennis shoe. Took quite a few chews, particularly for the little ones with only a few teeth right in front, to get them ready to swallow. My mother was the ace of the big oyster eating business. She just cut a few notches in them with her teeth to let out the flavor as they slid in and down.

Crabs

Keep the crabs alive until cooking time. A dead crab in the hot sun is a lot more dangerous than a live crab in the hot sun. They'll stay alive in a bucket of water only if you continually change it. If you are apt to forget, they keep better in a bucket with no water in it. Their gills can absorb oxygen from the air better than they can from stagnant water in a bucket full of other suffocating, urinating crabs. The best way to cut losses due to death is to let them have free run of the bilgewater in the bottom of a boat. Boil the crabs whole and alive in seawater. If the crabs have been in the same bucket for a while, rinse off the yellow urine before you put them in the boiling water. Don't get bit. A big blue crab will change your attitude about the apparent ease with which mankind exerts his domination over all living things. Them, yellow flies, no-see-ums, and mosquitoes have not learned proper respect for us quite yet.

When the crabs are red, drag the foot tub to the deepest hole of water you can find and dump them out—skip to the side to avoid the hot water. As soon as you can stand to hold them, pull the carapace off by prying up on the tip of the inlaid abdomen with your fingernail (or use a crab claw if your fingernails have gotten so soft that they won't work). Eat the "goody" out of the cavity in the middle of the crab. There are different kinds of goody:

One is the contents of the crop and stomach, which are encased in a little sack and extension sack right behind the teeth. It is usually pretty gritty with various kinds of stuff, but not usually sand. On seaside beaches, the grit is chewed-up shells of *Donax variabilis* (coquinas) and sand fleas (mole crabs, *Emerita sp.*), neither of which will hurt you. In marshes and creeks, the crabs (usually male) have been eating other crabs (usually fiddlers, *Uca sp.*) and oysters. Though it is possible that you might eat some carrion (maybe even a little bit of human being), my observations are that blue crabs mostly catch and eat live things. The contents of the crop and stomach of crawfish are a delicacy to the people (some elected officials) of Louisiana and crawfish are more indiscriminate than blue crabs. My own mother, rest her soul, always sucked that part up first. After I had learned the anatomy of crabs, I told her, "Momma, you know what that is you are eating?" "Yep," she said, "it's good." "That crab thought it was good when he ate it, too," said me. "Delicious," said she around a mouthful. Before you turn prissy and pass judgment, consider the hot dog and the hamburger. If you think, for a minute, that huge meat-packing conglomerates throw away tons of those nutritious and valuable things (ears, for a tame example) that, if wrapped in clear plastic and named by their real names, would send previously happy shoppers screaming from the store, you are wrong. Prissiness is a late-model invention in the evolution of mankind.

Another type of goody is the fat, which is a grayish white kind of stuff that (in a fat crab, and they all ain't) is right on top in the cavity and even extends out into the corner spines of the carapace, where it is easily dug out with the non-movable pincher of a claw. In male crabs, the fat is all mixed up with the gonads, which look like convoluted strands of spaghetti. Both the fat and the gonads are quite good and very nutritious.

Another type of goody is all that yellow crumbly stuff in female crabs who have not made a "sponge" yet. Those crumbs are the eggs and are my favorite kind of goody. Female crabs keep the eggs inside their carapaces until they are mature. Then they are moved outside under the flap-like abdomen, where the little larvae develop further. The eggs under the abdomen look like a sponge and have developed tough shells to protect the developing larvae. Make sure you don't throw the carapace of any non-sponge female crab away before you rake all that yellow goody out of the inside of the points of the spines. I think that the proof of what is good and what isn't is to try it on a child . . . one who hasn't been retarded by the *Froot Loop* and taught the word *yucky* yet. An ignorant baby will eat the yellow goody as fast as you can pick it out. While you are at it, eat those little muscles in the front of the carapace that move the eyes.

After you eat the goody, take off the dead man's fingers (gills, and like the sponge, absolutely inedible) and bite the legs off well into the body of the crab. You can teach yourself how far into the body to bite by experimenting with the paddle-shaped swimming legs. They should come off with a good bit of the "lump" meat attached. Eat that and any that is sticking out of the proximal joint of the walking legs. Do not throw those legs away. Any child with two opposing teeth can munch out a good piece of meat from the big joint, and in a pinch you can work it all the way to the toe. Clean out the big lump from the undivided swimmer fin hole. After that, it is sort of ticklish to get the meat from the walking leg holes in the body of the crab because there is a horizontal partition separating the pull-down muscle from the lift-up muscle. That is where small children get most of their shell from.

The claws are easy. Usually, if you bite the distal (outboard) side of each joint and then crack along with your teeth toward where the claw was attached to the crab, the meat will come out of each joint in one piece. Sometimes a crab has just shed and the claw is flimsy and damn near empty. We used to just chew the whole thing up and spit out what didn't go down easy.

The delicacy of this business is soft-shelled crabs. Usually, they are carried by their protective husbands. They find each other just before the time comes for the girl to molt into womanhood. The old boy holds her underneath him and carries her around until she molts. At that delicate time, he will eat your ass up if you mess with them. Though he can't help her shed her shell, he acts mighty anxious as he protects her. After she is all the way out, he mates with her while she is soft. Afterward, he carries her as before until she is hard enough to take care of herself. Somehow, all the girls in our crew have been thwarted in their efforts to find somebody to do them like that. Some of them, like my wife, have to protect the males that they wound up with—those who didn't get tired of it and run him off.

Soft crabs are best if rolled around in egg and buttermilk, battered with cracker crumbs, and fried, but we didn't have all that. We just boiled her along with her husband and the others while the anxious owner kept an eagle eye on the project. A fried soft crab is a special treat, but a boiled one ain't half bad. You just lift up the tips of the carapace enough to pull out the dead man's fingers and the teeth and eat her whole. One little girl in our crew used to specialize in soft crabs. While we were digging or fishing or messing around, she would continuously comb the grass for paired crabs. When she found some, she would put the male in the boat, but she didn't trust the soft female out of her clutches. It was a rare thing to see her when she wasn't guarding at least one soft crab in her hand. If the crab was caught early in the morning, a long way before boiling time, it would just get littler and littler while the girl carried her as she ate, first the claws, then the legs, and finally just a little of this and that for a snack. Once in a rare chance she would catch a gigantic soft-shelled male crab. At first we used to tease her and act like we wanted to steal her treasure, but her reaction was so fierce that we soon stopped.

Altogether, crabs are good for people. They teach caution, patience, politeness, and nutrition.

Baked Potatoes with Seawater and Oysters

Cut a cold, walked-on, bilgewater-soaked baked potato in half and mess up the middle enough so that an oyster won't slide off. Try not to eat the potato until you have opened at least one oyster. Put him in and sprinkle seawater to taste. Eat a little hole where the oyster was and then open another oyster. Soon you'll have an empty potato skin. Fill it with oysters and eat it whole in one big mouthful . . . don't talk or get tickled while you are doing this.

Baked Potatoes with Mustard (or any other kind of) Sardines

Do the same way with the sardines as with the oysters above. Eat a little and pour a little. Try to eke it out so that the sardines and potato even out in the end. Only a fool wastes the juice out of a sardine can.

Apples, Seawater, and Mustard

You guessed it . . . what can I say?

Under Watermelon

Slice and bust a large, hot watermelon into suitable-sized chunks and distribute according to the "Who shall have this?" ritual described in *Men Against the Sea* (Nordhoff & Hall; the second book in the *Mutiny on the Bounty* trilogy). Eat your part down to the green rind while you are completely underwater to escape mosquitoes, horseflies, yellow flies, and no-see-ums. Chew up and swallow the seeds, too—they scour the guts and promote good health. You can stick your lips up every now and then to get a little breath of air.

Crabs and Apples

Eat the crabs first and then the apples. Eat a goodly portion of the shell of the crabs and the core, seeds, and stem of the apples.

Crabs and Bananas

Gobble the banana while you are waiting for the crab water to boil. You can scrape the goody off the inside of the peeling with your bottom teeth, but don't eat the outside part. That won't do you a bit of good. Drink ice water to do you good and calm you down while you wait.

SAILFISH

in which someone else learns a lesson . . . well, almost

M Y FATHER LOVED boat kits. I guess he built ten or twenty or so during the time after WWII before he took off for California. When he found one he liked, he built the same boat over and over again and gave the finished boats away when the accumulation got out of hand. One of his favorites was some kind of canvas-covered skiff . . . just frames and a few stringers covered with canvas. Another was a tiny V-bottomed plywood pram that I believe was called a "Seashell." He was welcome to give either one of those away. The canvas boats were almost useless because you had to be so careful where you went and you couldn't drag it. The damned little pram acted just like damned little prams all do—slow, wet, and crank—and it could not be propelled with a paddle.

When I was about eleven, one of my sisters (the middle one,

then nine years old) and I took a trip down the Ochlocknee River from the Ga. 93 bridge to the Hadley Ferry . . . kind of short as the crow flies, but a hell of a long way as the pram is dragged. As soon as our ride drove off and we got out of sight of the bridge, the river dwindled to a logjammed trickle and the little engine (Elto "Pal") spat its spark plug out in the only deep hole in the whole river and was no pal to us from then on. The river was so low that we had to drag that pram and that little engine all the rest of the way. The trip would have been just a long wade through some mighty interesting country if it hadn't been for our water-craft. As it was, we wore all the paint off the keel and chines until all my father's little Reed and Princes shined like new money. My sons polished up the bottom of my old Grumman Sport Boat doing that same thing many years later, but enough of all that. I was going to tell you about the Sailfish when I started.

The Sailfish was a plywood kit, too. I never researched the design, but I believe that it was some sort of a predecessor to those ubiquitous fiberglass sailboards called Sunfish now . . . which, like an old .22 target rifle like the Boy Scouts use, is the standard to measure by when you think you have a hot-shot rig. A lowly Sun-fish sailed by a light, skillful kid in a good breeze will show just how much there is of that muchness you are so proud of.

So he built this Sailfish. I was about ten years old at the time and I got to sand the internal parts and paint the little plywood bulkheads and break off a few drill bits drilling the holes for the screws where he had stepped off some marks with dividers. He had this thing called a "Versamatic," which was a planetary screw-driving attachment for an electric drill. (His was a D-handled Black & Decker . . . ¼-inch chuck . . . weak . . . made a funny smell when it was running . . . made a real funny smell when I burnt it up trying to install a muffler cut-out on my momma's Ford station wagon forty-five years ago. I still have his old half-inch drill that stands knee high and won't drill a shaft log hole without extensive waiting periods between bouts with the spoon.) This Versamatic was a pretty good thing. It had two collars that spun when the drill was switched on. If you grabbed the top collar, the screwdriver bit sticking out of the end turned at a much-reduced speed to drive the screw, and if you grabbed the bottom collar, it backed them back out. Though the drill always ran the same speed, you could vary the speed and torque of the bit by letting the collar slip in your hand a little bit. I think the man who invented it must have been an old Model T mechanic, because that thing worked just like the planetary transmission in those old cars except that your hand took the place of the clutch bands. That old Versamatic was one of the things I wish my father had left when he took off for California about 1955. Oh well, at least he left the Yankee screwdriver, which would run rings around that gadget.

So we finished the kit. I believe there were a jillion little ¾-inch #6 Reed and Prince monell screws in the deck and bottom of that boat. I have to digress again at the mention of that. Like my father, I sure do love monel. You know, the invention of "stainless" steel sure wasn't much improvement over that wonderful maritime metal. If metal was wood, monel would be live oak. I guess it is too expensive to make stuff out of anymore and I guess it is too expensive to make stainless steel like the kind that they made the 1930 Model A radiator shell out of, too. Oh well . . . back to the Sailfish.

It looked just like a Sunfish except that it was made out of plywood. The mast step was the weak point in the boat. We children used to load ourselves out on the upwind side so many and so far and in such wind that the boat looked like it was heeling when actually the hull was level (and flying, too). We used to have to pull it up on the beach and take the drain plug out about every fifteen minutes and take turns blowing our breaths into the hole to build up some pressure inside the hull so the water would come out faster. When we did that, water would well up inside the mast step like a little spring. My father accused us of abusing his boat and tried to patch the mast step all different kinds of wondrous ways. After he took off for California, my mother finally fixed the damned thing with about a hundred pounds of concrete (glad I didn't have to drag it down the Ochlocknee River) and a bunch of coat hangers. After that, the mast had to twist the deck and bottom from chine to chine instead of just a little place in the middle, and it didn't leak quite as bad.

The Sailfish incident that has gone down in family legend doesn't have much to do with the boat, though. Right soon after the Sailfish was finished (before we children molested the mast step) my father was drinking a few martinis on the porch of the coasthouse with a bunch of visitors while the husband of one of those people was down trying to teach himself to sail. It didn't do to pass by on the beach in front of that house if you were not in the mood to be scrutinized and criticized. My father was pointing out all the things that this man was doing wrong to all the other observers on the porch and not only explaining the proper way to do them, but implying that anybody who did not have the innate intuition to already know which way the wind was blowing and how a single piece of cloth would act when presented to that wind in the way this poor man was repeatedly doing it was a fool. Indeed, I have made similar observations myself, but such verbal punishment was superfluous because the boat could take care of all that on its own. I don't believe that I have ever been involved with a boat that would hit you in the head any harder with the boom than that Sailfish. There is something about the geometry of the lateen rig, I guess. Of course, when you are sitting flat on the top of the slick deck with no real toehold and only about eighteen inches of clearance to hide in when the damned thing jibes, there ain't a hell of a lot that even the most agile among us could do but take the lick. This poor man took his share right there in front of the coasthouse audience.

As the slapstick became progressively more funny and my father's comments more acerbic, everyone failed to notice that the poor young man's young wife was not taking part in the mirth. While they, in the throes of hilarity, were sloshing gin with a little vermouth and sometimes an occasional olive over the rim of their little glasses, she was sitting still, the surface of her martini remained high and level and her olive stationary—even after she had set it down and taken up a five-cell flashlight, which she used to beat my father over the head until he was subdued. One witness to the incident said that she would have killed him if the lens hadn't busted and the reflector hadn't escaped and let the batteries out. I saw him when he got back from the hospital. The bandage was as big as a turban. I also fished the ruins of the flashlight out from under the settee. . . . Boy, was it ever dinged up around the threads of the big end . . . and some of the batteries were even dented.

Many years later, I used to ride the bus to California to visit my father at his house in Malibu (a trip just about equivalent to dragging a pram all the way down the Ochlocknee River except that there was no good place to go to the bathroom). One time, I was talking to one of his associates while he was outside barbecuing on the hibachi. The person told me that there had been a time in their association when things were said about life before California that seemed incredible even to a Californian. "Is that a fact?" said me. "Like all those little crescent-shaped bald spots all over his scalp. . . . Robb said that they were old wounds from back in his sailing days." "That's a fact," said me.

STORM BOAT MOTOR

*in which, due to the onset of puberty, I foolishly expand my
compulsion to include machinery*

BACK IN THE early fifties, people still thought that outboard
motors should be something that one person could carry
down and clamp on the stern of a boat all by himself. Of course,
they were beginning to fudge a little. My father had an Evinrude
thirty that I believe was the first electric start outboard motor in
the world. It would stagger him pretty good while he was waddling down to the boat with it in the deep sand. It was a silly
motor all around. Though it had a little vestigial electric starter
on it, it didn't have any generator, so after about two days, he
had to stagger back through the deep sand with the battery. Fortunately, the motor had a real recoil starter hidden under its cover,
but you had to open this silly little door to get to the starter rope.
Before the gremlins that eat all outboard motors had destroyed it,
the situation evolved down to where we left off the foolishness

with the battery . . . took the silly little door off and started the engine by hand. In spite of all this, I sort of liked that motor because in my speedy youth, it would trot the old Lyman pretty good and I thought it was hot stuff—at least until I saw my first storm boat motor. I was sixteen years old.

I had gone to this lake with the Lyman to show the girls and everybody else what was what when this guy launched a little plywood monstrosity with a big naked-style antique-looking outboard on the stern. I thought to myself, "Look-a-here at this piece of junk . . . let me blow him out of the water with my streamlined thirty-horse Evinrude Lark." When he got it in the water, the boat was so down by the stern from the weight of all that cast iron that the sheen of gas and oil from the foot threatened to follow the water in over the top of the transom. The man couldn't get back in the stern to go through the motions of starting this thing for fear of sinking, so he stood in the shallows while he did all his doings and wrapped the rope around the flywheel. Then he scrambled in, quickly pulled the rope before the whole business sank, and, when the motor fired, he scrambled forward to get to the steering wheel. The old motor started pooting smoke and hopping and jerking violently back and forth and began to almost run a little. The man sat there on the seat and clutched the steering wheel like he expected something to happen, and something did. The damn thing backfired four feet of smoky yellow flame from the front and a gout of blue smoke out the stern and seemed to explode. When the boat cleared the pall of smoke, it was already going about sixty (probably an accurate estimate from later experience). That man ran all over the lake with that thing. It bellowed like a bull and left such a sheen on the water that, if it had been these days, the Coast Guard would have sent the C-130. I kept the Lyman up there next to the grass. I didn't know that boats could go that fast. I decided to find out a little more about it.

Well, it was a storm boat motor. They were built by Evinrude for the government during World War Two. The intention was to propel a sacrificial landing craft (called a "storm boat") full of sacrificial men at planing speed on a one-way trip to storm the beach. Somehow, they figured out some other way to sacrifice the men, and when the war was over, there were a bunch of these old motors left and they were sold cheap as surplus. Some people made little race cars out of them and some were fool enough to actually put them on boats.

I had found the source. That man had about twenty-five of them, all in their original wood boxes complete with propellers, spare parts, instruction manuals, and carrying (yeah, right) handles. He was ready to let one get away from him, too. He showed me how to cut them down to size (they were very long in the foot in the original configuration), repitch the propeller (the gear ratio was about one to one—needed more pitch for a little boat), drill two big holes in the muffler to let out the noise . . . and mix the gas (I might be wrong, but it seems to me that it was one quart of fifty-weight motor oil to the gallon) to make the sheen that was always in the water around one of those old motors.

It was a peculiar outboard compared to what we are used to now. I guess it was an offshoot of the old two-cylinder opposed engines of the thirties. A storm boat motor was four-cylinder opposed, two-stroke cycle. It acted more like a two-cylinder engine because both the cylinders on each side fired together. The reason for the four cylinders (I was told) was because the pistons would be too big to cool properly in the center if the motor had only had two cylinders and they were trying to build the biggest two-stroke engine they could. To enhance the spark for starting, there was a doohickey that shorted out the two plugs on the port side, so when it first started, it was actually running like a one-cylinder engine—a real rough-running one-cylinder engine. It had a side-to-side snatch to it that would break the arm of anyone who tried to interfere.

The starting ritual was like this: First, you opened the gas shut-off and the vent on the cap of the gravity-feed gas tank. Then you retarded the spark (necessary if you wanted to stay in the boat with the pull rope), wrapped the rope in the flywheel groove, and hit the primer pump on the carburetor a certain number of strokes according to the temperature of the engine and the air. Then you opened the throttle wide, waited for your knees to quit knocking, and gave a hell of a pull. If you had figured the number of priming strokes right, the engine would start. If it didn't, you could hit the primer again and take a chance on flooding the crankcase, which required all four plugs to come out and be dried off and the flywheel spun enough to clear the gas from the crankcase and cylinders (that's where part of the sheen of gas that accompanied these engines came from). Cranking one of them was a matter of intuition, brute strength, dedication, and reckless desperation.

After the engine started (running on the two starboard cylinders), you had to quickly advance the spark, stand to one side, and hit the wildly gyrating doohickey that let the electricity into the portside plugs. There was no neutral. She was already under way, and you better get your ass under way for the steering wheel so that if the two portside plugs weren't fouled, you could outrun the quart of flaming gasoline that belched from the carburetor when those two cylinders went to work. And so you could be in a position to try to steer when the boat hit the water after the initial leap. After that, it was just plain loud stinking joy for a little while. The engine wouldn't run at anything much less than full throttle without fouling the plugs, so you had to let it eat, and eat it did. There were some storm boat motor men who could manipulate the independent spark and throttle enough to get it to go at half speed for a little while in an emergency, but nobody could make one idle. For me, it was wide open all the time—at least until the gas gave out. When that happened, the silence was deafening. The old motor would sit back there stinking and sizzling water and frying oil, just daring you to pour some more gas in the tank.

I had a girlfriend back then. She was not the one I married and was not built for that kind of duty. She got kind of disgruntled after I had whipped black, greasy streaks from that stinking gas-soaked starter rope on her yellow bathing suit and naked hide over and over again trying to crank the storm boat motor. I had a feeling that the end of our relationship was near. Finally, we went on a trip down the Suwannee River. I had gotten to be pretty good at running that thing by then and we didn't have any bad trouble until the bar that held the two steering cable pulleys vibrated off the back of the motor (*vibrate* ain't exactly the right word) and the thing kicked all the way over and popped the top board off the transom and came in the boat with us, bellowing like a bull and biting like an alligator. It was hard to get one of the sons of bitches to start and hard to get this one to stop. By the time I finally managed to find a way to stop it without losing my hand, it had gnawed up the whole stern of the boat and was hopping on its flywheel up front after us. My girlfriend and me had to walk about ten miles up the riverbank back to the boat ramp to get the car. The skeeters ate that girl up, too. She gave me up after that—she eventually married a chiropractor and, as far as I know, has never set foot in a boat again.

I kept my storm boat motor for years on a sawhorse out under the lumber shed. I told myself that I was going to build just the perfect boat for it one of these days, but one day I was out there looking for a board when I smelled an old familiar stench. It seems that the termites had finally eaten one of the legs of the sawhorse clean off and pitched that old bastard, carburetor down, into the dirt. A tiny bit of the ancient essence had dribbled out. I just left her lay. I guess I just ain't the man I used to be. Oh well.

HOW I BECAME A BOATBUILDER

*in which I take a wife, turn professional,
and learn a lot all at the same time*

I GUESS MY FATHER started me off. He was a boat fiend and a writer . . . a good writer who wrote books about boats and people who built boats. I read them when I was little and got so enthusiastic that I couldn't help myself. It began a compulsion that has lasted all my life.

It is easy to train eager children. All you have to do is watch them until you see them doing something you want them to do and marvel at it. (It has to be the real thing, though; you can't fool yourself into thinking that your children like something just because you want them to, and you can't fool *them* into thinking that you are really marveling when actually you are a little disappointed.) My father had the formula down perfectly.

First, he would write a good book about boats and children and send it off to the publisher. When the check came, he would take off on a long trip to find out something else to write about. I would stay home and read the book and build me a boat so I could be like the kids in the book. After a while, he would come home and marvel at the boat that I had built. He would marvel in earnest, too, not because the boat was so wonderful, but just because I had built it. He couldn't build any kind of a boat himself from scratch (could handle a kit fine) and it impressed him to see a ragged-assed little cattywampus thing nailed up out of plain old boards floating in the pond on our place. The reason he couldn't build boats (he was a pretty good house carpenter) was because he couldn't sharpen edged tools, not to save his life. But he could write and he could marvel.

I can remember my first edged tool perfectly. I have it in my tool cabinet beside my big English slick in case I need it. Its little blade is just about worn half in two. They called it a Christy knife, and I guess the name was copyrighted. It had one little limber blade that slid back into the steel wire handle when you worked its button with your fingernail. It wasn't much (my apologies to Mr. or Ms. Christy), but it was marvelous in my hands. I was just a little preschool kid when one of my uncles sent it to me for Christmas during World War Two. Momma quickly slipped out the back door with it as soon as she could and dulled it on the brick steps so I wouldn't cut the fool out of myself. Little did she know that I watched the process carefully from the bushes. As soon as she was through and I had my knife and a little privacy, I determinedly ground the edge right back on it on the very same brick. I cut down fifty feet of pittosporum hedge the first day and wore a regular groove in that brick. When my father came home from the war, he just marveled.

I was a filthy-footed, gritty little boy. I stayed so dirty that people in my family wouldn't let me in the house except for occasions special enough to wash me off out on the steps. I used to have to eat my dinner on the steps with my brick. The men who worked on the place used to bring strangers to see me and make me show them my Christy knife. First the visitor would look at it and laugh, then he would feel the little worn blade. I tried to teach my father how to sharpen. He couldn't seem to get the knack, thought it must be the brick. He went to the hardware store and bought the biggest and best double-sided Norton stone they had (twelve by three, I still have it, worn almost half in two like the knife). It was much quicker than the brick, but the results were the same—I could but he couldn't. I sent him a Lansky device just before he died, but I guess he was too old and shaky by then, because it didn't work either. If he hadn't discovered X-Acto knives back in the fifties, he would have been helpless. I wish he could have seen all these disposable-blade tools they have now.

So I built a bunch of boats when I was a child by the chopping, carving, and nailing method. I used plain old black tar to caulk them with, and they made me wash off with kerosene before I could come in the house to sleep. The smell of kerosene still makes me feel adventurous even after fifty years.

I took down the whole chicken house for lumber (probably seven or eight hundred board feet of virgin cypress five-quarter by twelves). I chopped stems out of firewood with a five-pound axe (a sharp axe is a useful tool). Every now and then, one of those old waterlogged flat-bottomed boats will fill with methane from the bottom and ooze to the surface of one of the ponds on the place for a little while. My granddaughter will show her little friend.

"My granddaddy built that when he was a little boy." "Yeah? But what *is* it?" It will let out a big poot of pond gas and settle to the bottom for another fifty years. The little girls will stand on the dam and marvel. One of those old boats is the nucleus of a two-acre floating island in the biggest pond. Not long ago, I tried to rob some of the wood off it, but it was grown in so tight with willow roots that I couldn't. Besides, an alligator tried to eat me while I was out there.

After I grew up (sort of), I joined the Navy so I could see about some bigger and better boats. Sure as hell, they stationed me in Puerto Rico on shore duty. I was disappointed at first, but my ramblings soon disclosed that I had been dumped right in the middle of the masters of the chopping, carving, and nailing boatbuilding method. When all the other fellas at the Naval Station jumped in the público and headed for the museums and art galleries on Luna Street in San Juan, I jumped on my motor scooter and went to the little town on the water right close to the Naval Station where the masters were.

I had been introduced to this little town by my Mexican roommate when I was a mess cook. He was always broke from sending money home to his family in Mexico and didn't have the público fare to San Juan. He still liked to hang around the museums and art galleries, so he rode on the back of my scooter and showed the way to this bar in a little playa. I sat at the bar and nursed my tiny Corona (that's Puerto Rican Corona . . . different from the high-priced Mexican import so popular with the yuppies), while he tried to talk a little noise to the young girls and their dueñas. I soon got bored with that and went out on the patio facing the sea. This bar was built right exactly on the water's edge. Moored fifteen feet from the jukebox, shining in the neon lights, was the prettiest sailboat I ever saw in my then limited life (and I ain't seen too many any prettier since, either). I came back in the daytime.

I was a real young-looking, innocent little fella back then, and the old lady at the bar liked me fine. Soon I had interrogated out the facts about the boat in my pitiful Spanish. It belonged to Julio and he had built it right beside the bar and he was right out there this minute building another one. I went straight to see what was what, and sure enough, there was Julio with some other men sitting on some logs playing dominoes. There was the beautiful skeleton of a boat standing with its sternpost almost in the water on some little posts. I (with my flat-bottomed experience) marveled. Julio was not impressed with me, neither were his friends. I had the feeling that they had seen all the young sailors they wanted to, but I couldn't bring myself to leave. I sort of hung around and looked at the boats and the water and the side wall of the bar, against which they peed. The domino game went on until dark and some beer came from the bar and some little bowls of something that smelled real, real good. I decided to go inside and try to find the source and I did. It was some rice with beans and some kind of gravy on top. I thought that it was the best thing I ever ate in my life, and I vowed to stay in Puerto Rico forever, eat rice and beans, build boats, and learn how to play dominoes.

To make a long story short, I hung around the bar all the time. Finally Julio grudgingly allowed me to step and fetch from the bar and pull and wrassle rollers when they were pulling boats out. (They pulled some very big boats out right beside the bar using nothing but the same little logs that they sat on to play dominoes and a little pushing and pulling, and some discussion.)

I earned myself a name because I thought if I showed them how sharp my pocketknife was, they would marvel like the people back home and let me be one of them. They didn't marvel, but they did name me "El Cuchillo," which I took to mean "The Knife." I was so out of touch with everything else but the business beside the bar that I didn't know that Bobby Darin had just sung that song about the other man with a knife and that it was very popular on the jukebox. Later, amid many chortles my name was shortened to just "Mack." It was bad timing altogether.

Strong compulsions run deep in my family and I hung on through thick and thin at the bar. Things were pretty slack at the Naval Station back in the leisurely fifties, particularly in the galley where I was still a mess cook. Mess cooks aren't real cooks, just some temporary help that other outfits send to help out, usually as a disciplinary measure (they call it "KP" in the Army). My tenure as mess cook wasn't because I was bad, just that I was inconvenient. The Navy had spent a lot of money sending me through this big-deal weapons school (where I excelled, if I do say so myself) only to find, when I had to take the physical examination before I entered the swimming phase of the school at the end of the program, that I was color-blind. I asked them what the hell that had to do with swimming, since, as a result of my previous experience as a boatbuilder, I could swim like a fish (pulling a sunk boat, no less). They said that color blindness made it impossible for me to be what they had trained me to be. I never figured it out and neither did the Navy. Here I knew all this secret crap and couldn't be sequestered with all the other hotshots that knew the same thing so they could keep an eye on me to be sure I wasn't playing into the hands of the Russians. The Navy's solution to this was that I stayed a mess cook for longer than anybody else in the world, while they tried to figure out what to do and while I went to the doctor once a week to see if my congenital color blindness was any better or not. My solution was to buy me an old motor scooter (Sears Allstate Vespa) so that I could poot off to the bar where the boats were built between meals at the galley. Meanwhile I attempted to memorize the sequence of the cards in the Ishehara color-blind test.

I got to be such a fixture down at the bar that every now and then, they would let me debark logs with a dull shovel and maybe scrape bottom paint or unload lumber and logs if they were in a good mood. I watched everything like a hawk and I was sure that I already had all the skill to do it, too. All I needed was to understand the method and get to where I could eyeball the shape like Julio.

They didn't have any complicated tools. Most of the cutting was done with an axe and a machete. They used an axe like a slick to back out the inside of planking. They hardly ever sawed anything. Planking was ripped from boards of resinous Caribbean pine by nicking the edge to the line with a machete and then chopping off the blocks between the nicks. Keels and all the other deadwood parts were just plain chopped out of Caribbean pine logs with a regular chopping axe. Sometimes they would use a machete like a drawknife or a scraper to smooth something up. It is easy to get the impression that this was a slipshod business from this description, but it wasn't at all. The boats that Julio built were beautiful. The planking was as smooth and fair as anything ever touched by sandpaper. The chopped-out Madeira mahogany frames were beveled to fit the planking better than any tilting arbor bandsaw could have done it (and better than many big-name stateside yachts). They made all the hardware right on the beach out of car springs and other salvaged stuff. Some of it was sent to San Juan to be galvanized, but most of the time, it went right on the boat like it came from the charcoal forge after being painted (a forge prepares steel for paint just as well as a sandblaster). Julio could make a perfect mast band in about fifteen minutes if the forge was already hot. They inlet a short piece of chain into the masthead and drove the top band down over it for a place to hook the halyards and shrouds. All the shrouds were three parts of galvanized single-strand wire that they twisted into a cable. There were no turnbuckles or even lanyards. They just drove a spike between the lay of the wire and twisted the shrouds up tight (I guess that's where the term "Spanish Windlass" comes from). I have had a good many boats rigged like that since. It is sort of nice to know that water is not freezing in your swaged fitting down there at the dock in January, or that your fifty-dollar emergency stay-end fixing kit ain't still home when you are down around Cuba and one of the nineteen strands of your backstay sticks its tongue out at you. There is something to be said for that kind of hardware. Half an automobile leaf spring with the eye still on the end makes a real trustworthy chainplate.

I watched and learned a lot from Julio and the others, but I never was allowed to really participate and they never got to see how well I could chop and carve and drive nails. I found out later that these men weren't discriminating against me because I was a sailor-boy or foreigner at all. There was just a rigid tradition in their art that young poots like me weren't allowed to touch edged tools to wood. They also believed that derision fostered the development of humility and character. I was just too young for boatbuilding—or dominoes. I should have been glad, because I found out later that I wasn't as good as I thought I was with edged tools and the masters wouldn't have marveled at all the miss-licks I made with the axe and the crossgrain splinters I pulled up with the knife and the machete. There was one thing I could do, though: I could pee higher on the wall than any of them.

Nothing lasts forever. After I got off mess cooking and made enough rank, I went home on leave and found out that I had become mature enough to be attractive to and attracted by the little Reynolds crew girl that hung around my sister, so I took her back to Puerto Rico with me. We bought one of Julio's oldest boats with her first allotment check ($137.10 got us the *Nueva Eva,* nineteen feet) and took it around to the Naval Station and tied it up in the little marina. Every Saturday, we would go down there and run rings around all the other boats the naval officers had. One of them hired an architect from St. Croix to take the lines off the *Nueva Eva,* and he confided in me. "Captain Bridgers don't know it, but there are hundreds of these kinds of boats and all of them will sail like hell. I ought not to take his money, but I will."

I set up building boats in our little house on the Rio Blanco river halfway up the side of El Yunque. I didn't have the ability to find and cut the Madeira ("Majaguilla") trees for frames and I didn't know where the keels and planking came from, so I ordered plywood (¼-inch five-ply, marine) through Rasmusen Hardware and glue (Weldwood) and screws (Everdure monel, a wonderful thing) from Defender Industries and started building plywood boats when I wasn't working on secret stuff for the Navy. I sort of had a captive audience. The Navy wouldn't ship a boat for enlisted men like they would a car or household appliances, so the only way those people at the Naval Station could get a boat was from somebody like Julio or me, and Julio's boats weren't what everybody wanted. We, like so many, were infatuated with plywood boats. It was a mistake. I actually believe that the widespread acceptance of plywood as a boatbuilding material was just as responsible for the notion that wood is not the best material for small boats as the invention of fiberglass and the development of cheap aluminum boats. There just aren't any old plywood boats that have seen much use.

My mother-in-law sent me a book by somebody named Chappelle (I still have it, worn almost half in two) and I marveled. I learned to loft on the front porch of our house. I hope the full-sized lines of that beautiful little Hampton boat are still under a little paint on that concrete slab.

When the time came for me to get out of the Navy, I cashed in my savings and ordered a bunch of tools from Sears, Roebuck to be sent back home so I could set up shop and be a successful boatbuilder. Soon after we got home, fiberglass was just hitting its stride and you could buy an aluminum butt-head skiff (now appropriately called a "Honkey Drownder") from the discount store for $59.95. I wound up painting houses, working at the trailer factory, furniture factory, and all sorts of things in the early years so I could afford to build boats. Fortunately, there were always enough customers to keep me going—if I could build the boat cheap enough. I remember building a decked, marine plywood, double-ended sixteen-foot duckboat with a steam bent oval coaming for $75. Years later, a man used it for the plugs (hull and deck) to make a chopper-gun fiberglass version that was pretty popular around here for a while before they relaxed the no-airboat-and-outboard-motor rules during duck season. I have talked to old boatbuilders who were put out of business by aluminum and fiberglass, and they said that it wasn't the superiority of the material that ruined the wood boat business but the cheapness. If it hadn't been for the commercial fishermen (who have never liked fiberglass boats, let alone aluminum around here) and a few die-hard discriminating people, the wood boat business would have died completely out in the North Gulf of Mexico in the sixties.

I went through all the stages: plywood (I quit that about '67 except for one or two single-boat lapses), bent-frame carvel, sawed-frame extra heavy duty Caribbean style, and strip-planked boats built from all sorts of lumber. I built one extra-light cold-molded boat from sawed veneer and epoxy when it first came out (a nasty business). Now I mostly build lap-strake boats even lighter than that—and Caribbean style, natural crook framed, heart-pine planked sailing smacks.

Did I ever go back to good old Puerto Rico to see if things were still the same? I am sort of scared to. They might put me back on mess cooking, and besides, I still don't know how to play dominoes. What happened to the girl I hauled down there and back? I still got her. Worn about half in two, but she is still ready to get in the boat.

A Note About the Boats of Puerto Rico

The boats of Puerto Rico were inside-ballasted sloops built sort of like the boats of Bermuda, the Bahamas, Cuba, and on down the Caribbean. The frames were chopped from the little Madeira mahogany trees that are becoming so scarce now on the Greater Antilles and Bahamas. Even in the fifties, black mangrove was substituted, particularly for repairs. The boats were very long-lasting, although it was sort of like the story about George Washington's axe. Some of them had three new sets of planking and two sets of frames. The deadwood, transoms, and planking of boats that I saw were always made of very dense Caribbean pitch pine (*Pinus elliottii*, variety, *densa*), and some of those parts seemed very old indeed.

By the time I came along, all of the fishermen used outboard motors, but most of them kept the old sails and rudders for their boats in the house in case of hard times. Though the only sailing Puerto Rican boats that I saw, except for the *Nueva Eva,* were big schooners on their last legs and a few little builder's jewels like Julio's own little boat, boats were built to sail. Though they weren't usually sailed, they were all built like sailboats. There is deep water all around Puerto Rico and fishing there is an open-sea proposition. Outboard motors probably made the fisherman's life a little easier, but it was no place for the cheap, flat-bottomed skiffs that took over the inshore fisheries in a lot of other places with shallow flats and bays.

These boats were all different from one another and from other Caribbean models, but they had some things in common. The keel was straight on the bottom and there was very little drag to the stern. Puerto Rican boats had straight stems with a good bit of rake. The stems had just enough curvature in profile to keep them from looking concave. The rabbet was straight. The forefoot was extremely hollow. The builders went to a lot of trouble to carve and bend the hard pine garboard strakes into as much distress as the wood could stand so as to accentuate this hollow; indeed, some of the garboard strakes were split trying to do this. The splits were opened up and beveled with the tip of a machete and caulked just like any other seam. The builders tried to build a lot of flare into the bow and the boats always had voluptuous cheeks. One of the advantages of building by eye is that the builder can alter the shape to accommodate the tolerance of the particular boards on the job. The body of the boat had almost straight deadrise into a pretty hard bilge. Sometimes, the floors had a slight bit of hollow as the planking approached the keel, particularly in the garboard strakes, but the floors were never convex. The run was very flat and the deadrise of the transom was either flat or slightly hollow. The old *Nueva Eva* would lay over and plane on this flat run (one reason for her ability to outrun the modern cruisers and daysailers at the Naval Station). The wide transoms were heart shaped with a good rake, unlike the transoms of boats from some of the former British colonies.

The rig was an extremely long-boomed jibhead main with a small jib. The boom stuck way out behind the transom and the first reef was just to tie this off with a lanyard. The mainsail was laced both to the boom and the mast, and there was no board or club at the peak like in some island boats. The *Nueva Eva* had way more sail than any other nineteen-foot boat I ever saw (another reason for her success at the Naval Station). I never measured anything, but her mast was tall and her boom was long. The jib was sort of small. Sometimes, in light wind and a head chop, she would not come about unless we backed this little jib, but the old boat could be easily balanced to self-sail in any forward wind by adjusting the jibsheets. The rudder just lollygagged behind the boat without being lashed when she was trimmed right. I eyeball-built a replica of her in 1965 that would do the same thing.

I believe that the longevity of these boats was due to the heart-pine planking and deadwood and the single-sawn Madeira frames (double-sawn frames in open boats don't hold up well in the tropics). Though the bottoms were painted a different color from the rest of the boat, copper bottom paint was not usually used. The bottom paint (usually bright blue) had a distinctive downturn of the boot top up by the stem, which accentuated the hollow forefoot.

The boats were commonly pulled from the water on rollers. When a fisherman came in, everybody on the beach would lend a hand. It was not unusual for a helper, sort of incapacitated by age or drink, to get himself run over by the rollers in the soft coral sand. After she was out, one of the floorboards would be wedged under the rail and there she would sit on the rollers until it was time to go out again. The people would sit in the bar and admire her; discuss what they would do differently if they were to build themselves one—and eat rice and beans and play dominoes and listen to Bobby Darin on the jukebox. Dang . . . the good old days.

TERRIBLE TORQUE AND
THE FLOORBOARD MAN

in which there is a terrible tragedy,
so you might want to skip this one

Just before I went back to Georgia to get married, it got to where I was spending so much time down at the bar where Julio and them built the boats that I became acquainted with other people in the little town. There was a little drugstore there and the owner and his wife were very kind to me. They had one table where they served various meals to a few people. It was almost like being invited for supper to eat there. Since there was only one table, the customers all sat together and, since the town was so small, they all knew one another. Little old lonesome me was attracted to such as that, and the women of Puerto Rico were very nice. I guess the men were, too, but they were so aloof that it was hard to tell. I ate supper there all the time and it got to where the women would give me a little taste off their plates and I learned that Puerto Rican cuisine was a hell of a lot more than just the delicious rice and beans that had become the staple of my diet.

Julio had just finished planking up a most beautiful boat and I had been on mess cooking so long by then that I had a little clout with the cooks and bakers who ran the galley, so I was able to wigglework my schedule and I could get on my scooter and show up at the bar most anytime I wanted to. Though I was far too shy to speak the language except in emergencies, I had learned to understand a good little bit of Spanish . . . particularly the language of boats. I think the taciturn Julio and the others might have surreptitiously helped me a little bit by speaking slower and enunciating a little more carefully. Anyway, I had watched the painting man scrape the seams, where the caulking iron had frazzled the edges of the planks on the already fair hull of the new boat, with what looked like a piece of glass from a TV picture tube. There was a tradition of subcontracting in the building of the boat. Julio always set up the deadwood and the few initial frames that served as the molds, and he beveled the transom and cut the rabbet in the stem (there was no rabbet on the keel, the heavy, stiff Caribbean pine garboard strakes just bore on a bevel) and he was always elbowing right in the middle of the crowd when the garboard strakes were forced to comply with the notions of his eye, but most of the rest of the boat was built by subcontractors who just drifted in when the time came. I learned to listen to the discussion about when who was supposed to arrive and learned a good little bit about the social life of those people, too.

The man who subcontracted to fit the intermediate frames and floors to the already planked hull was very fat and seemingly slow. His work was truly an astonishing thing. There wasn't enough room on the beach by the bar to accumulate the enormous pile of wood that you see around every other boatshop I have ever been in (mine is beginning to cascade), so all the raw material for each job was brought in on Julio's big flatbed truck. You ought to have seen what the frame man had to work with. They backed the truck right up to the boat so El Gordo could climb, snorting and puffing like a bull, up onto the bed with a whole truckload of what looked to be a jumble of gnarled limbs straight out of the forest of Hansel and Gretel. Like so many of the operations of building a plank-on-frame boat by old professionals, all that chaos was carefully ordered and the frame man knew exactly which of the crooks he needed and where it was supposed to fit after he had chopped the bark off and shaped and beveled it by eye using a little hatchet and a chopping block on the stern of the truck. He was so good that he seldom had to adjust either the curve or the bevel after he had tried the futtock for fit. He had a little nickel-plated, all-steel Stanley Yankee push drill in his hip pocket, and after he had drilled the holes through the planking to fasten the frame, he would position it and buck it with a sledge hammer head. I tried my best to detect the signal that summoned one of the others to come drive the nails when he was ready, but couldn't. At first I thought it might have been a grunt, but he grunted all the time. It must have been subliminal.

Anyway, that was what it was like down by the beach. Up in the bar and at the drugstore, the social life was even more interesting. I had already committed myself to going back home to Georgia to find out more about that girl who had been writing to me, so my interest in the young girls of that town was like that of a casual observer. You know respectable (and there weren't any other kind in that place) Spanish people have a rigid set of customs about the courtship of their young girls. Though it is perfectly permissible for girls as young as thirteen to go to the bar where alcohol is drunk and gambling is occurring, they may not go alone. Some old dueña has to go with them. Even though the old gal might have been well into her dotage, her eagle eye made sure that there was no hanky-panky to the tune of the jukebox. Nevertheless, love was fallen into and proper liaisons were set up under the rigidity of that system—a system into which came a newcomer. Not me, Terrible Torque.

Here is what happened to Terrible Torque. I finally got off of mess cooking and went to work at the secret shop where I was supposed to be. By then, I had taken the test and passed into what they called "third class petty officer," and even though I was brand-new at the shop, I outranked a good many of the old hands including Terrible Torque. I hate to let this out, but you know, intelligence, experience, and ability have nothing to do with the hierarchy of the enlisted men of the Navy. Rank is established simply by taking a little abstract and mostly irrelevant written test. Though I had never actually seen a WWII steam-driven torpedo and such a thing had nothing whatsoever to do with the job for which I was trained, how that weapon worked was the basis of the tests I took to advance myself through the Navy, and a marvelous machine it must have been . . . right up my alley. I'll briefly describe its mode of propulsion. Oxygen and alcohol were injected into a heavy-duty steel flask, where they were ignited and burned with an astonishing fury. Water was sprayed into this hellhole and the unbelievably powerful jet of steam that resulted drove a tiny turbine to generate a horsepower more like the result of an explosion than the propulsive efforts of machinery. Though the steam pressure was so high and the vapor so hot that the turbine blades were quickly eroded, the torpedo was a one-shot device and durability was not a factor in its design. I don't remember figures exactly, but the whole engine of the thing wasn't much bigger than a two-gallon bucket and put out many hundreds of horsepower. I was so fascinated that I, a mess cook, quickly became the youngest third class petty officer in the U.S. Navy.

Terrible Torque earned his name because he was sent (not by me, thank goodness) to the battery locker to put a little water in the batteries that we perpetually maintained so, in case the Russians were to break bad, we could whip their asses. There were zillions of bucks worth of batteries in the battery locker. I know the technology of secret batteries has made great progress since 1959, but I still wouldn't want to let any cats out of the bag, so I will just tell you that one of the ingredients of the plates of some of those batteries was sterling silver. Anyhow, the way you added water to them was to unscrew all the little plastic caps and, using a syringe, fill the cells up exactly like you used to do a car battery before the manufacturers worked that scam called "maintenance-free," which, if you can figure out how to take the plastic caps off, you can add a little water to maintain one of those to last much longer than its intended lifespan. So Terrible Torque took all those caps off and filled up all those batteries, and it took most of the day. When he got through, he read the checklist, which said, "After all the cells are filled, replace the caps and torque them to fifty-inch pounds using torque wrench Mk 5, Mod 3." Terrible Torque finished the job and came into the little office room and lounge where we hung out most of the time.

"Man, I sure will be glad when I make third class and don't have to do that shitty job anymore," he proclaimed, glaring at me.

"Well, it's over with now. You won't have to do it again for thirty days," said the chief. "I hope you didn't just screw the caps on and not torque them like Gasparetti used to do, because I am sure gonna spot-check your young ass."

"Yeah, I torqued them but I couldn't get no fifty-foot pounds on any of them," explained Terrible Torque. It turned out that he had stripped the plastic threads on every single plug on eighteen quadrillion bucks worth of batteries, which had to be destroyed and disposed of in a ritual that was mind-boggling in its extremity. In case the ridiculousness of this narrative has you confused, there is a big difference between the torque of fifty-inch pounds and fifty-*foot* pounds . . . a terrible difference.

Terrible Torque was a nice young man. The whole thing was the Navy's fault. They ought to have had better sense than to put two different fifties on a torque wrench.

Anyway, Torque had gotten conned into having a certain pretty large portion of his paycheck deducted into government bonds. Not only that, but he had committed himself to make exorbitant payments on an enormous gilt Bible and some other publications that were sold by a well-organized cadre of rapacious old chief petty officers. In short, he didn't have the car-fare money to go to San Juan to visit the art galleries and museums on Luna Street like all the other single-pukes at the shop, so he rode on the back of my scooter to the bar on the beach, where he sat and listened to the music. It didn't take him long to notice the young girls sitting demurely with their dueñas. Old Torque became more and more mesmerized. He asked me how it was done to get to talk to one of those girls. "Well," I opined, "probably the first step would be to learn a little Spanish." "Hell, man, I can't do that right now," he wailed, "can't you just teach me one or two words just to get me started." "Well, okay, just go over there to her and say '¿Baile?'" After he had practiced the word and got the inflection of the question right, he gathered his gumption and walked over where the girl who had caught his eye sat with her snoozing grandmother and said his word. With that, she was in his arms and they were dancing to "Just a Closer Walk with Thee."

I can see that this story is fixing to get ponderous if I keep on like this, so I'll cut it to the nub. Language proved to be no barrier to Torque and the daughter of the people who owned the drugstore. For one thing, she spoke excellent standard English; for another, true love has no need for speech. It was pure, proper euphoria (the best kind) around that little town. Torque and the girl progressed rapidly through the ritual. Kisses and hand holding were permitted, but not much. If they got to sighing too loud, the ever-present old dueña would wake up and "no, no, no." Finally an agreement was reached and Torque cashed in his government bonds and bought a plane ticket to take the girl and her grandmother to Miami to meet his parents. I hate to tell you this. I think it is the most pitiful thing I ever heard of. They came right back. It turned out that Terrible Torque's mother and father thought the girl was a little too dark to suit them. The grandmother and the girl got right back on the plane and flew back to Puerto Rico. Torque stayed on to argue and whine for a while, but to no avail. The young couple never saw each other again, and though the people in the town still tolerated me, they were kind of reserved acting after that. Both Torque and the girl were the saddest-looking kind of people for all the rest of the time I knew them. I think their hearts are still broken to this day.

After something like that, it is hard to concentrate, but I'll try to tell about the floorboard man. I don't know if you know this, but fitting floorboards in a round bilged boat is some tricky business and, though I didn't know that either, I still had my doubts about the floorboard man. He was so old that Julio had to help him into the boat. By then, it was complete except for the rigging and the floorboards. The white hull gleamed like a beauty there on the edge of the Caribbean Sea. I don't remember the exact color of that particular boat, but Puerto Rican smacks are always tricked out in bright colors from the rub rail up. This one might have had the sheer strake painted bright yellow with blue rail and cap. I know that the boot-top was bright blue and had the distinctive downcurve as the hollow of the forefoot approached the stem that is so characteristic of the boats of that region (and which will still bring tears to my eyes when I see it in a picture or my mind's eye). I have seen a lot of small carvel planked boats and it might just be nostalgia, but none of them have been as pretty as Julio's. That ain't got nothing to do with the floorboard man. I was just trying to set the scene of what it looked like while he was at work. He must have been much respected, because everybody was very helpful. He stood in the boat or sat on the seat and folks handed the wood up to him. Using just a machete and a claw hammer, he chopped the strakes of the floorboard so that they fit around the frames exactly. You know, in a fishing boat, the floorboards have to fit tight or the bait or the fish might get in the bilge and get lost in the rocks of the ballast. He had a little chopping block on the seat beside him to back up the plank as he drove the machete blade into the crossgrain for the frame notches with his hammer, but he cut the beveled curve that fit the planking by holding the board across his knee. I watched carefully as he chopped little notches along the edge and then popped off the chunks between with the machete. He hit close up by the handle and the inertia of the long blade beyond carried the sharp steel through the wood. He had a little triangular file with which he touched up his blade. He had all the floorboards fitted by mid-afternoon and the men helped him out of the boat and into the bar, where I guess they talked quietly over their tiny Coronas and rice and beans. I wouldn't know, though, because I couldn't leave the boat. It was such a piece of work.

MONKEY ISLAND

in which I leave my young bride for . . . monkeys

Aﬅer my wife and I got married in January 1961, we rented a little one-room concrete house halfway up El Yunque near Río Blanco, about twenty miles from the Naval Station. My mother, though she, like the Navy, didn't approve of us getting married so young (my wife was just seventeen), felt like we needed a car, so she shipped an old ragged Volkswagen down there for a wedding present. We did need a car. I had a motor scooter, and while it was an easy ride down the mountain to the Navy, it was a pretty hard pull for that little thing with its .410 gauge tailpipe, coming back with both of us and all the groceries from the Navy Exchange. We didn't need the Volkswagen for that, though. We needed it to sell so we could afford to buy Julio's own precious jewel of a sailboat. You know, if your boat isn't too pretty to walk away from without looking back, you ain't getting all the goody out of life, and I can walk away from any automobile.

I think that long haul up the mountain did that scooter good . . . might have burnt the smut off the spark plug. It always ran much better after that, particularly after I started hauling plywood on it, too . . . which made for a pretty sporty trip, especially that part on the tall bridge across Río Blanco. Sometimes, when the wind was right, it was hard to decide if it was rolling, flying, or fixing to swim. You can call that sort of thing irresponsible if you want to, but I have been trying all the rest of my life to get back to that status. Two boats, no car, and a seventeen-year-old girl on the back of my motor scooter to help me hold the plywood. How can responsibility compete with that?

Well, that exact situation didn't last too long; we sold the old *Nueva Eva*. Julio's jewel (*Rosa*, twelve feet) was such a joy that we never used the big boat. I have found that to have been the proof to a pretty good rule. I call it the "rule of joy." Simply put, it says, "The important thing ain't comfort, it's joy." Joy in boats is inverse to their size. When they get big and full of engines, batteries, toilets, stoves, and other comforts, there just ain't as much room for joy. All those things are like a bunch of relatives that vote wrong. Not only can they cancel out the good you are trying to do, they can beat you, and there is nothing you can do about it. The little *Rosa*, though . . . whooo. Memory is sort of selective and I might be forgetting a little misery, but if there was any, it was quickly pushed out of that little boat by the joy . . . no room.

The peacetime Navy ain't no (I hope I'm not letting any cat out of the bag) real hard job and we had plenty of time to sail all over the paradise that eastern Puerto Rico was in those days. There were uninhabited islands everywhere. Some of them belonged to the Navy and had the abandoned remains of old World War Two buildings on them. One old rotting-down barracks building looked like nobody had been in it since the guys moved out. There was still a picture of Lana Turner hanging on the wall. Even Vieques and Culebra didn't have hardly anybody on them. Those were so far away that, though we started out once, we never made it all that way. Jane was pregnant by then, and the ground swell was so big that, while we did fine on top of the waves, there wasn't any wind down in the bottoms and she didn't like it down there. Finally we turned back after we topped one wave and saw a destroyer that hadn't been there when we were on top of the previous wave. I remember noticing that it was so close that we could see the little clear circles in the windows of the bridge where the spinners were slinging off the water from the spray that was flying from the bow clear across the whole superstructure as the ship tore through the big even swells (there was no water at all coming in our boat, which brings us back to the previous comparison). We never did get around to trying another trip to Vieques and Culebra. We had plenty to do sailing to the many little islands near the shore.

I remember the first one we went to, Cayo Santiago, off the coast opposite Humacao. We could see it from where we moored the little *Rosa* beside the bar in Naguabo Playa. One day, early in all these adventures, we packed our lunch (Gouda cheese, long bread, Clorox jug of water, and two apples), hopped on the scooter, rode to the bar, waded out to the boat, and sailed to that island. It was an interesting-looking thing to flatwoods children like us ... high, heavily wooded, and rocky. After we got close, we could see a tiny cove with a little coral sand beach. By the time we managed to beat in there, we noticed that there was a metallic clang coming from back in the woods somewhere. There wasn't a regular rhythm to it like machinery, but it was happening often and it was loud. It sort of made us worried about landing in the little cove, but we had sailed all that way and were itching to scramble all over that island and see what was what. Finally we worked the boat up where it was shallow enough to wade ashore and I took the tiller (majaguilla, dense and hard) so I would have an edge in any negotiations with whoever was making all that noise. As soon as we put the first foot on the beach, such a swarm of big monkeys came out of the bushes and trees and started screaming and hopping up and down and gnashing their terrible teeth so loud that no negotiations were possible. We did a little hopping ourselves and ate our bread and cheese in the boat while we sailed around the island.

Though we didn't get to swim in the freshwater pools and take a little nap in the shade, we did find out the source of all the loud banging. Those monkeys must have belonged to somebody, because they were eating out of a plain old steel Dumpster. A monkey had to open the lid and get in, and slam the lid behind him, to get something to eat. We noticed that some of them had short-looking tails for Rhesus monkeys (which is what they were) and assumed that those were the slowest. After a while, the in-monkey would raise the lid and get out of the Dumpster or another monkey would raise the lid and get in and chase him out. It took at least two bangs for each monkey to get a little snack. They were eating something that looked just exactly like what we used to call "big-turd" hog feed. One would come out of the Dumpster holding as

k a long time. It was hot and stormy-looking, too, and by the
e we finally got in range of the island, I was beginning to feel
I was earning that twenty. Not only that, but, just as we rowed
into the little cove, a hell of a thunderstorm came up. The wind
ipped down on us and the rain burned like a bunch of slingshot
ks. Fortunately, the cove gave us some protection from the
ves, but the bottom was rocky and the anchor didn't want to
ld. It was shallow, so we jumped out to hold the boat until the
rm blew by. At least it was shallow back at my end. Old union
an went in, over his head, in a hole. By the time he had scram-
ed halfway back in the boat, we had drifted to where he could
and up, too, but he still wasn't comfortable because it was
lowing cold rain like hell . . . felt like it was fixing to hail . . . and
e had lost his flip-flops when he fell in the hole.

We held the boat for what seemed like three hours. We squat-
ed in its lee to keep the rain from stinging quite as much of us
nd to hide from the lightning that was flashing all around. Fi-
ally, it let up enough so we could talk a little and then we could
see the island and the little beach. "Let's get this monkey business
over with so I can take that twenty bucks of yours. I think I saw
a bar back there where we got in the boat," he said, mincing
ashore in his bare feet on the rocky bottom. I was beginning to
worry, because I hadn't heard a single clang from the Dumpster
in all that time. Maybe they had taken the whole monkey crop to
the auction just like we used to do hogs. By the time we got anchored and waded up to the beach, I was feeling my soggy twenty-
dollar bill for maybe the last time because there were no monkeys
anywhere. Usually, they would be hopping and screaming by the
time we entered the cove. "Where are my damn shower shoes?"

many of those big pellets in his mouth, feet, and
and still work the lid. As soon as the outgoing
ground, the lid would slam and all his friends wo
and take his hog feed pellets away. It was kind
we always stopped by there to drift and watch
on our way to the other islands that lay beyond th
always very careful not to drift too close for fea
monkeys would come take *our* hog feed away fro

Although I didn't have to do much, I did have
at the Navy. I had a friend who worked in the s
had one of those antagonistic friendships that me
though they never have anything nice to say to ea
are still buddies. This guy was from Michigan and
long line of dedicated steel mill and automobile fac
men. Our experiences were so different that we had
teresting things to explain. I had never seen a union
and I was curious and listened to what he said with
had never seen hog feed or a possum, so he listened to
too. The main difference was that I had read about f
unions and knew the Jimmy Hoffa news of the tin
buddy's experiences were pretty believable to me. He
was pulling his leg with my alligators, armadillos, fifty-
fish, and things like that because he was ignorant. He
lieve the Monkey Island story at all . . . called me a bul

Finally the ribbing about it got involved with money
was made. To save my dignity, one Saturday, I had to
wife home and take this joker to see the damned monke
planning to make a quick trip, but it was the time of ye
the trade wind is not absolutely reliable like it usually i

demanded the money winner. "They ought to be right here on this beach." With that, I heard the sound of a thousand-monkey fight way back in the woods. "Hear that, union man?" says me. "Them's monkeys and they sound like they are on their way down here to collect their union dues. Let's us get back in the boat while I collect my dues." "I ain't going no goshdurn-where until I find my foolish shoes," said he in the traditional language of the enlisted Navy man of that time (a language in which I became very proficient in only four years . . . if I do say so myself).

In spite of all that bravado, he did have to leave without his shoes when all one thousand of those monkeys came running down to the beach. I was already in the boat when the first ones appeared from out of the trees, and I got to watch the other fella realize he had lost his money and then decide to abandon the search for his shoes. We both pushed the boat off into deeper water and watched the monkeys. They ran out of the woods for ten minutes. Apparently they had been occupied doing something interesting way back in the bushes during the storm and didn't find out that there was something more interesting to do on the beach until just now. I wondered what could have been more important to them than eating us up until I saw the king monkey strut out of the trees. It looked like he had been in some kind of bad monkey fight. He looked like he was mighty proud of those shower shoes he was wearing, too.

SEAGULL

in which I learn not to be so gullible

WHEN I WENT home from Puerto Rico to get married, I was able to catch a hop in an old P2V anti-submarine plane to Mayport just across the St. Johns from Jacksonville. She was coming to meet me, so I wore my best whites and spit-shined my shoes. I had to sit back in some makeshift quarters and my whites got so filthy that after inspecting me, the marine in Mayport almost refused to let me out of the gate. Not only that, but the bomb bay where I rode was unheated and I like to have froze to death. Not only that, but the flight crew played a cruel trick on me. They told me, as the only occupant of the bomb bay, that it was my duty to announce to the forward part of the plane that the bomb bay was "all secure, sir" after we got off the ground. I was to lift the lid to this little tube and holler this information down in there as soon as the plane leveled out at cruising altitude. When I finished doing that and looked up, the entire crew, including both pilots, was standing in the door laughing and slapping their thighs. I thought I saw the world passing by down through that little tube and it seemed to me that it smelled strongly of urine. Oh well . . . one a minute, P.T. said. I guess, now that they have women on air crews, they have a dishpan welded on that thing to make all opportunities equal.

After we got married, we flew back to Puerto Rico on a regular airliner (Pan American, Lockheed Super Constellation . . . bathroom accommodations not so concise). Jane had a bunch of things that she needed to take, like her clothes and some cooking utensils and stuff, but we had to leave most of her belongings behind so that we could take the outboard motor. It was a wonderful little two-cylinder, three-horse, weedless Evinrude (made in Belgium in 1954) that I had worked for a long, long time unloading boxcars of chicken feed to get the money to buy. It turned out that we should have taken the other stuff on the plane with us. The little three was too short in the shaft and too puny in the propeller to do much with the old *Nueva Eva*. Though it wasn't suited for that duty, it has always been a delight on the little narrow skiffs that I use it on now. Yep, I still got it.

As soon as we got settled down in our little house, I set up building boats in the one room where we cooked, ate, and slept, and started making a little spare change. We saved up and bought a brand-new British Seagull—a five-hp, five-blade wheel, brass gas tank, "Silver Century Plus," made in Poole, Dorset, in 1959. Dubbed by its maker "The Best Outboard Motor for the World," that engine showed us what that "Plus" meant the first time we

fired it up on the transom of the old *Nueva Eva*. We were astonished. The old boat cut through the water like a destroyer. We
made a bunch of expeditions up rivers, into mangrove swamps
and bays where we had never been able to go before because of
certain preferences of the boat's for wind sort of coming from the
side or behind and certain preferences of ours away from rowing
in stifling heat and biting bugs when there was no wind coming
from the side or behind. Though we appreciated the extra mobil-
ity, we soon found that the real joy of the expedition came when
we were able to shut the damn Seagull down. When it was running, it was sort of intrusive. First, it made a lot of noise. A Weed
Eater, chainsaw, or even a wretched Jet Ski ain't nothing compared
with a British Seagull at full bleat. Second, it made a pall of smoke
that seemed to wad up behind the transom of the boat and then
curl up and jump on us like some djinni gone bonkers. There was
a certain vibration, too. We found that it was necessary to completely break contact with the boat in order to steady our eyes
so we could see the sights when the engine was running. We
learned to time our levitation to coincide with the gaps in the
pall of smoke. I especially hated the carburetor of that Seagull. It
had this little tin choke that pivoted into a little cut in the throat
of the thing from the outside. You had to choke the damned engine to start it even if it was hot. It would start, though, and
continue to run with the choke closed, but it skipped much
worse than normal and the resulting violent snatching made it
almost impossible to grab the crazily wiggling choke without either getting tangled up with the flywheel or getting the hell
burned out of you by the hot engine (the damn thing got hot all
the way from the water to the gasoline). Not only that but it

slung a large slobber of oily gas out of the gaps in the carburetor all over you while you were trying to catch the choke on the
fly. If the engine was cold, not only was it necessary to fight the
choke, but you had to push down on this little leaky button on
top of the float bowl, which depressed the float against its will
and allowed the carburetor to flood the crankcase with enough
gasoline to start the engine (or a DC-3).

We were young and excitable, though, and hardship was just
the predecessor to joy for us. We tried to wear that old Seagull
out. I even tried to improve it a little bit, and about the only
successful one of these experiments was a fuel pump I machined
up on Navy time so we could quit having to pour gas into the hot
engine every time it ran out. I don't have to tell you that, when
we got out of the Navy, we brought the old Seagull (and the Evinrude three and a Wilcox Crittenden thirty-pound yachtsman anchor) home. As soon as I could, I built a copy of the old *Nueva
Eva*. We clamped the Seagull on the stern, spread a little gas
around, and commenced exploration of the Gulf of Mexico.
Though we could always count on the old Seagull to crank and
run, it was sort of like how you can always count on income tax
time. Along with the regular disgusting behavior of the thing, we
had some interesting mishaps. Once, while we were still in Puerto
Rico, it spat out the "sparking plug." I knew something was
wrong because the engine began to hit every lick instead of every
other lick like it usually did when it was easing along (we never
ran it wide open for various reasons). When I looked back to see
what was what, I saw the spark plug on the end of the wire swinging back and forth with the violent wiggle of the engine like the
tail of a dog who is real glad to see you. Just as the engine

blew so much of the gas out of the hole that it no longer had the excess it required to run, the spark plug was flung off the wire and plummeted to the bottom of the clear water. So did I—found it immediately. Back home when that happened, in the muddy Apalachicola River, I could not find the plug. It was a strange-looking, big-thread thing, not commonly available in stores—or at least that is what I thought—so I machined an adapter and ran it on an old Volkswagen plug. Then one day I was messing around in the Western Auto looking for this and that when I saw a British Seagull spark plug. Of course, the box said that it was supposed to go in a Model T Ford. I thought that was pretty appropriate. After we had had the old engine for a long time (seemed like forever) we were coming in the pass between St. George and Dog Island with a fair wind against a falling tide. In those conditions, when the water running out of the bay through the pass encounters the wind blowing in from the sea, the resulting conflict makes for great, big, almost stationary waves. I had the old engine running to sort of help us through. When we hit the first of those waves, the boat pitched up and the engine pitched off the stern at the same time. The silence was delightful. We said "too bad" and sailed on through the pass as if nothing had happened, but after we were inside, I noticed that the boat didn't seem to be acting quite right. Turns out that the old Seagull was porpoising along behind on the gas line. I had it running again before we went into the river.

The diurnal alternation of the sea-breeze, land-breeze situation is very pronounced in the summertime in the near-shore Gulf of Mexico. The sea breeze begins to pick up just about exactly when the morning starts to get uncomfortably hot and the land breeze comes right after dark. Both of them are pretty predictable and wonderfully welcome. Old-time sailors knew this and, along with the tides, worked it to their advantage. As you know, the phenomenon is caused by convection from whichever surface—sea or land—is hotter at the time. Any wet, rising air condenses as it encounters the coolness of the upper troposphere, and that makes thunderstorms and rain . . . out to sea at night and over land during the day. There is nothing more sweet-smelling than a land breeze coming out of the wet woods across an island or a boat.

One dead calm evening, we were coming back from Waccasassa Bay across the Gulf when the fair land breeze made up. We began to smell a hint of the fresh, rained-on woods of the land mixed in with the exhaust of the old Seagull. The sails tightened up, the boat heeled a little and began to sail on the tack she loved so well. I shut the Seagull off. When I pulled the pin and let her slip into Davy Jones's locker, I could see my wife nod just the slightest little bit.

Epilogue

One time I had to buy a part that had vibrated (we say "viberated") off the old Seagull. Of course we had bought the engine from a yacht store in San Juan. But since we did not remember the address of that place, I wrote to the address on the gas cap: "British Seagull, Poole, Dorset, England." I am afraid that I explained things too much in that letter. As a result, the part came immediately, and a lady there became a pen pal of mine. She was part owner and main captain of one of the "Little Ships" of Dunkirk. She had a garden in her backyard and we exchanged *Brassica* seeds for many years until she died about 1985. I heard that the "Best Outboard for the World" is now being built by Pakistanis. I give them joy of each and every one.

PRAMS

in which I become a successful,
professional boatbuilder first shot out of the box

B Y THE TIME we were settled down in our tiny house on El Yunque, I had made up my mind to go ahead and be a professional boatbuilder. I ordered something called *Boatbuilders Handbook* from Weston Farmer's wonderful *Science and Mechanics Magazine* and built an eight-foot V-bottomed plywood pram from plans in the book . . . well, sort of like the plans in the book. This boat was supposed to be for rowing only and had small transoms both bow and stern. Outboard dependence had already become established by then, so I modified the design so that it had a big transom at the stern to float the outboard and the sailor. My wife and I built a bunch of them and sold them as fast as we could build them for eighty bucks each, unpainted . . . which suited me just fine. The sailors all wanted to paint them themselves and I think they stole the paint from the Navy, because there were a lot of gray prams circulating around the big harbor. We had a captive bunch of customers because it was almost impossible to buy a cheap boat in Puerto Rico in those days. Even an old Puerto Rican plank-on-frame boat cost hundreds of dollars.

I think we hit our peak of production, two prams a week, just before our first son was born. Our normal pace was a pram a week, but we usually took the weekends off to go sailing. When the time for the baby to be born came close, we thought we ought to hang close to the scooter on weekends so we were able to slap another pram together on those two days. Jane was driving screws with a Yankee screwdriver when the first contraction came.

Which, those prams were built without the benefit of electricity. I ripped the plywood with a handsaw (you hold the handsaw upside down and walk forward with it—try it sometime), drilled the holes with a hand drill (which I still have), and drove the screws with the wonderful Stanley Yankee spiral ratchet screwdriver (which, in the right hands, will hold its own with any rechargeable driver drill and will beat it with big screws). I planed the bevels with the same secondhand block plane I use now. The plywood (five ply, quarter inch, marine—three sheets to two boats) came from Rasmusen Hardware Co. in St. Croix, who arranged shipment to their branch in Naguabo on the mailboat. I ordered the screws (#6 by 1-inch straight slot, flathead, Everdure monell . . . such a wonderful metal . . . such beautiful little screws) from Defender Industries in New York . . . the Weldwood glue too. The Puerto Rican mahogany for keels, chines, seats, and transom frames came from a little sawmill right down the road and was delivered on a big truck in rough bark-to-bark flitches of variable thickness. I made the transom frames out of the wigglesome edges that I ripped off to get something straight for the keel, chines, and seats. I planed all that with the block plane—made a man out of me—made a pretty nice pram for eighty bucks, too, if I do say so myself. I wonder if there are any of them still moseying around down there in that beautiful place. I still have the plans and the old tools and the same woman. Now all I need is a stack of that five-ply plywood, a pile of those mahogany flitches, some of those beautiful little screws, and a bunch of captive customers.

I made enough money doing that to order a bunch of tools from Sears, Roebuck to be sent to Georgia so I could be set up to continue in that profitable business when I got out of the Navy. I figured I could manufacture those prams and one or two other economical boats and make a good living. The baby and my walking papers came about the same time. It was raining like hell the whole trip down the mountain on the scooter to the Navy hospital.

When we got back to the states with our new little son, we found that every discount store in the world had a nested stack of aluminum skiffs ten feet high . . . $59.95. I couldn't build a boat as cheap as that.

I wound up doing a bunch of other stuff . . . painting houses, building cabinets and furniture, working in factories and on tugboats and commercial fishing boats. Hell, I even went to college and became an oceanographer. Taught eighth grade general science for ten years, but I built boats all that time. I built a nineteen-foot, cypress, eyeball copy of the *Nueva Eva* while I was carrying twenty quarter hours worth of college work and supervising a night crew at a furniture factory. I finally gave up completely on plywood about 1967 or so and quit trying to compete with factory prices. My two sons were raised in the shavings and helped from the time they were old enough to poke a rivet in a hole. As the years went by, their participation has varied from being full- or part-time partners to being just full-time kibitzers as usual. One of their contributions to the business is an edict that I can't build any more unprofitable boats unless they get first dibs. There was a brief lapse in this policy when the youngest son, then thirty-five, decided to come in with me full-time and try to make a go of the business. We shook all the vacillating prospects out of the bushes by lowering the price, and though we gave some mighty nice presents to some pretty oblivious people (and some who weren't), he was only able to hang on by the skin of his teeth for four years before his shoeless children became social outcasts at school and he had to go back to his schoolteaching job to make a living. I was pretty lonesome in the shop after that, but now those shoeless children are sticking rivets in the holes and rolling around in the shavings. Life is a circular thing, ain't it?

PLEISTOCENE CREEK

*in which I almost give it all up and
quit the boatbuilding business for good*

I HAVE A COUSIN, a little younger than I am, from whom I was inseparable until I joined the Navy. We even invented our own language in which we were both named "Old Eeen." We did a lot of wild things together when we were boys, and his folks said that I was the one who always instigated the worst of those things. After I got out of the Navy, I continued to try to push up some kind of insurrection in the Old Eeen.

One of the things we did when we were boys was to try to live off the "fat of the land" back in the Ochlocknee River swamp like we were some of the wild people of long ago. The land back there, though isolated and wild enough, wasn't as fat to two little new-boys as it had been to the long-gone old hands who had left their sign along the banks of the river. We did manage to live like wild things for weeks at a time, but we were some hard-bitten, filthy, and very hungry little boogers when we finally made the decision to give it up and walk the five miles out to see if there were any cinnamon rolls in the pantry.

I got out of the Navy just before President Kennedy got shot. On that day I had just finished restoring an old bandsaw and I cried on the freshly polished table . . . rusted it up. Not only that, but I found that the Old Eeen had grown up. I was anxious to go wild again, but the Old Eeen was always remodeling the bathroom or hanging Venetian blinds or fooling with his car or some other civilized domestic chore. I missed him, but that didn't keep me out of the bushes, swamps, and wild coastline around where we live. On one of my explorations, I found Pleistocene Creek.

I was down there at the coast messing around in the marshes and rocky shallows where, if you can ignore the contrails of the jets heading to cursed Tallahassee, it is possible to imagine that nothing has changed since the old days. I noticed that in some of the little marsh creeks, even on the rising tide, the water seemed to be running out and it seemed to be a little bit fresh tasting. I wondered if some of those little streams might actually be distributaries of undiscovered rivers that flowed from the abundant limestone cave-springs, which, when the sea level was lower, were home to the people of the Pleistocene . . . the hunters of the mighty mastodon and the long-haired mammoth, eaters of the colossal *Megatherion* and giant bison, savage competition for the great bears and terrible cats whose bones are found around the ancient fireplaces, wonderfully preserved in the cave-springs ever since the ice-age time. Those are the same springs that made the short little rivers that still bear the names that the people gave them so many thousands of years ago. After the ice melted back about where it is now and the sea came back, the water table rose and filled the caves. The people lived along the banks of the old rivers and spoke the ancient names. These were the cheerful catchers of the lowly oyster, pinfish, blue crab, mullet, scallop, and Seminole killifish, the durable parts of which show up in the kitchen middens from only a thousand years ago. These were the same happy folks who were run off by worried fools like us who roar thoughtlessly around in high-powered machines and don't even know the name of the place where we are or see what it is like . . . people who would starve to death like ignorant pilgrims if they were set down naked in the middle of all that.

Late one fall, I took my lightest little boat way back in the marsh and let myself become stranded by a low spring tide when the north wind blew the water even farther away from the land. Tasting the trickles, I dragged the boat through the little marsh creeks all through the mud and over the rocks and oyster bars looking for a stream running fresh water. It was hard work. When it got to be dark, I squatted in the low tide mud and savagely ate my raw pelecypod snack and lay my skeeter and no-see-um bitten self down in the bottom of my tiny boat, where it was grounded solid in the mud of the creek that I was working my way up right then. Before daylight, I was awakened by the wind singing in the trees—trees that weren't there when I went to sleep.

I found out that the wind had shifted around to the southeast, the tide had turned, and the combination had done, in just a few hours, what I had been trying to do, off and on, for a long, long time. I was drifting in my tiny boat, spinning slowly in the current of a small, limestone-banked river so far from highways, boat landings, and houses, and so hard to get to that it was easy to convince myself that I was the first person to see it since the wild people. After it got to be daylight, I could see what it was like—a concise, deep little river maybe thirty feet wide. The solution-hole-riddled limestone banks were almost vertical and there was a layer of black loam overhanging the rock walls. The woods on either side were higher than anything I had seen along this section of the coast. There was an overstory of cabbage palm, red cedar, and live oak trees. Except for scattered palmettos, a few yaupon (*Ilex vomitoria*) bushes and leaves, the ground was shaded bare. I could see taller trees farther back from the river which might have been ash, tulip poplar, swamp hickory (*H. aquatica*), *Magnolia grandiflora*, red bay, and laurel oak. Some places on the bank and little ponds off the river were lower than the rest, and there were short, big bald-cypress trees and tupelo. There was a generations-old osprey nest in a cypress snag right on the edge of the creek. It was easy to see potsherds sticking out of the dirt along the bank and on the bottom in the shallow nooks of the river. I saw two shell middens that looked untouched since the last person had dumped the last basket of shells a thousand years ago. Though I longed to start looking further, I knew better. Those things didn't belong to me, and besides, the tide was already getting ready to go out. I paddled with it, looking at the landmarks as best I could, and went to get the Old Eeen.

Things in the modern world are always more complicated than they ought to be and it was a long time before I could get back to that place. My wife and I had two little boys by then, so I was working all week at a paying job and the boatbuilding business took all my weekends. I guess I sort of joined the Old Eeen in the real world for a while. I didn't have time to paddle for days, sleeping in the bottom of the boat at night, just to get to the memorized spot to go into the marsh. One of the outboard skiffs that has become so indispensable to me now would get me down the coast to the go-in place, but that wouldn't have suited my romantic notions, so I put it off until I had the time to paddle all that long, long way. Neither me nor the Old Eeen had time to do things right anymore. That wonderful place was just as safe from us as it was from the TV football fans for a long time.

Finally I managed to shake loose one January when I got laid off at the furniture factory where I was working at that time. I called the Old Eeen. He was just getting ready to paint the house and fix the gutters, but I browbeat him into putting it off for a little while since it was so cold. On the way down in the car, I told him about that place for the first time. I painted a pretty picture, too. Then I said "Eeen . . . we could go wild again. We could stay wild this time. Nobody in the world knows about that place but me. It ain't on the quadrangles and you can't even see it from an airplane. Even if they knew, nobody will drag a boat all that way just to get to a little creek . . . too far from the TV. You could just not show up in your classroom on Monday morning. The doings of the world would get along just fine without either one of us. Your wife could get along just fine without you and, Lord knows, mine's would soar like an eagle if she could drop this old heavy load. We could go back there and just set this damned skiffboat adrift. This norther would take it to Cuba. Somebody would be delighted to find it washed up. We could dug us out a canoe and live off the fat of the land forever. Wouldn't ever have to worry about no insurance or nothing." The Old Eeen sat silently over there on his side trying to act like he was looking out the fogged-up window. "We could be real savages, too, like the unconquered Calusas," I went on. "We could paddle swiftly but silently out of the marsh in our canoe . . . keep our heads down out of sight behind the grass . . . then we could swoop down on those fishing boats out on the flats, slip up behind them before they knew what was happening, and knock them in the head with a lighter'd knot. We could drink all the beer out of their icebox and smoke up their cigars and then send their boat on off to Cuba, too. Nobody would ever know . . . 'lost at sea.' " The Old Eeen's eyes darted around a little bit, but he still sat there silently. Finally, he reached in his pocket and got him a cigar and gave me one, too. After he got it lit and smoking good, he said, "Eeen, what if there were some women in that boat?" "Well," I said, "if they were plump with pulchritude and cheerful-looking, we could take them back to the creek and indoctrinate them into our ways and smoke up their Kents. If they were mean and bossy-looking, we would just knock them in the head, too." "I ain't too crazy about that," he said, looking worried. "Maybe we could tell in advance? You got your knobblers, ain't you, Eeen? We could spy on them from the marsh grass and just pass up any boat with mean-looking women in it. I wouldn't want to knock no woman in the head." "Naw, Eeen," I scolded. "You cain't have no knobblers back in the naked wild woods. Hell, you cain't even have no matches." "Yeah, but we could light them Viceroys with a coal when we got back to our fire," said the Old Eeen, eagerly smoking hard on his cigar.

Things don't always turn out right, even with the best of plans. Like I said, this creek was a long, long way down the coast from the nearest road. After we had launched the skiffboat at the closest possible place, we had to hurry so we would have time to pole in and take a brief look at that wonderful little place and then make the long, long trip back to the boat ramp before nightfall because that sort of country is not navigable in the dark.

While we were tearing along in the calm, shallow water in the outboard skiff in the north-wind lee of the marsh, I hit a perverse conch (*Busycon perversa*) shell with the foot of the motor and sheared the pin in the propeller. It was freezing cold, so even though the water was shallow enough to get out on the flats to pull the wheel, I decided to lean over the stern to do it. After I got the propeller off, damned if the engine didn't tilt down and flip me over the transom, out of the boat, flat on my back in the cold, cold water. Not only did I get saturated wet, but I disjointed my right middle finger (never did get completely well and sometimes makes people think that I am attempting some sort of communication) and dropped the durn propeller nut and we couldn't find it to save our lives. We had to turn around right there and row all those miles back to the boat ramp. If the Old Eeen hadn't had on two pairs of britches, I would have froze to death.

Epilogue

I can't remember if the Old Eeen and I ever managed to get back to that little creek. When my sons got old enough to be interested in that kind of thing, my family went back and carefully camped on the ancient bank right where I knew the old people had last slept a thousand years ago. After it was dark, it seems like we heard their spirits out in the woods. Next day, my oldest son and I swam all the way to the little spring that was the headwaters for most of the little river. The clear water bubbled up through big-grained white sand and thousands of salamander larvae and eggs. The banks were thick with poison ivy and other terrible bushes and vines. It was the wildest little place I ever saw. Sometimes we talk about going back, but the boys are grown men now, just about in the same fix as the Old Eeen. I haven't been back there in twenty years. I am sure that the population explosion around here since then has not let even that spot go undiscovered by the damned go-anywhere airboats, Jet Skis, "go Devils," and other such joy-riding travesties that are so popular among the ignorant and thoughtless. Both my children and the Old Eeen's are long grown up. He is still a schoolteacher—has all Christmas vacation off. He finished digging a pond in his yard and sold his backhoe and I noticed that his house was all painted up and the roof looks sort of new—well maintained. I am just as no-count as I ever was. We are both so old now that the dilemma about what to do with the women has solved itself. We'll just knock them all in the head. What the hell did I do with my phone number book?

SHEEPHEAD HEAD SOUP

*in which there are the natural histories of two fish
and a worm and . . . yet another recipe*

B ACK IN THE mid-sixties while I was in college, I worked for
this mad researcher who was trying to eradicate corn earworms on the island of St. Croix. He figured, if he could do that,
then he would know just what it would take to do it to the whole
American continent, where corn earworms are the number one
agricultural pest. I won't go all into it, but corn earworms don't
confine themselves to the hairy end of corn, but eat tomatoes,
tobacco, soybeans, and almost anything else. If it hadn't been for
corn earworms, there would have been no need for all that DDT.

At first I lived with the entomologist who was pushing this
project, but his family was due to arrive as soon as the school
summer vacation started back in the States, so I moved out into a
little derelict trailer that was on some land owned by a resident
biologist at the experiment station. I wasn't sorry to leave, either.

Though he was nice, the man with the grant didn't want to talk about anything but corn earworms, and the only thing he ever ate was peanut butter sandwiches. I moved to where the conversation was interesting and the food was exquisite, and I'll get to that here in a minute. There were two of those trailers in an old abandoned mango plantation on top of a high hill. Mine wasn't level but, fortunately, the wall side of the bed was down so I wouldn't roll out. Sleeping for a little time was all I needed to do in there. The only trouble was that I would wake up in the middle of the night and imagine that the damn thing had gotten a flat tire on the low side and was fixing to tumble down the hill into the Caribbean Sea.

The other trailer had been fixed up pretty good. The occupants had leveled it up and hooked up the electricity. The people who rented that one were Manny and Ivan. They were there in St. Croix working on the building boom that they had before those terrorists shot those golfers down at Fountain Valley and put the quietus on tourism in St. Croix, maybe forever. Manny was from St. Martin on the French side and Ivan was from Saba. Back in the sixties, though a man could eke out a living on those islands (and from the sea), there was no way to make any money, so industrious men from all over the Lesser Antilles went someplace to work for as long as they could stand to stay away from home.

Ivan was lonesome. He showed me photographs of his family and his little house and farm. He had a sweet-looking, bashful wife and two sweet-looking, bashful girls, and a very small house on the windward side (indeed, in the town of Windward Side) of the mountain. You know, Saba is an interesting-looking place. It is an extinct (we hope) volcano and the only level ground is in the bottom of the crater (indeed, the town of Bottom). Ivan's house was jacked up in the front about twelve feet and was clinging to the cliff with the back side. He had a little white picket fence about a foot from the road and about a foot from the front of the house. There was no room for any steps, so they had to climb up to the back door from the road. But there was room for his little bashful crew to stand looking over the fence at the camera so Ivan would have something to remember them by while he was working in St. Croix to better their situation. He remembered them, too, I tell you. I think he was weighing the value of this money he was making.

Manny was a different kind of man. Though he had a wife and what looked like about twelve children back on the French side (you know, St. Martin belongs half to France and half to the Netherlands, and ain't neither one got much), he also had a girl-friend in Christiansted. I never met the woman, but sometimes Manny would come home to the trailer and take a quick little dip and doll himself up with so much perfume that I don't see how he could keep his eyes open to drive. He had a car. He had spent some of that money he was supposed to take home to his wife and shoeless children on a car. It was an old Volkswagen and I rode to town with him once. Not only was the perfume just about deadly, but Manny couldn't drive worth a flip. I mean, the man had no notion that a car could be turned over. He didn't pay attention to where he was going or to what the car was doing. He was always wandering from one ditch to the other. If it hadn't been so dangerous, it would have been comical. It was as if he never realized where he was heading until he got there, then, when he felt the tires drop off the pavement, he would get very surprised and snatch the wheel, then drive contentedly over on the other side and hit that ditch. And he changed gears the same way. He would start off in first and, when the poor car got to going as fast as it would go in that gear, he would peer down at the accelerator pedal (one of those with the roller for your foot) and mash a little harder, peer at it some more, mash some more, then get a surprised look on his face and begin to peer at the gearshift lever and clutch. Finally he would change gears and act very satisfied with himself until he realized that the car had stopped accelerating again. Damned thing had four gears. It was a trip. My first trip in that car was my last, but I don't think Ivan knew any better, because he had never ridden in any other car but Manny's.

Ivan and Manny worked only six days a week (pouring concrete for a new hotel, now empty) but I had to work seven. The completion of my day's work was a borderline business, I tell you. I had to check these little sticky moth traps (you know corn earworms are the caterpillars of a moth, *Heliothis zea*) every day and there was one on every square mile of the island. I had this old tore-up, raggedy Ford station wagon that the researcher had leased, and I drove it all over the place full of these horribly sticky traps (I kept a rag hanging out of the gas hole to wipe my hands). If I started before daylight and drove like a bat out of hell and ran through the bushes like a wild hog to change out traps, I could barely get through in time to catch five or six hours of sleep before it was time to haul ass again. I had to eat peanut butter sandwiches on the run.

On Sunday, Manny and Ivan drove in Manny's car to the rocky cliffs on the Fredericksted end of the island and climbed down and caught parrot fish on their handlines. You know, the people of the Caribbean don't fool with reels and rods. They just buy a spool of about twenty-pound monofilament and slip a big lead on the end of the line, tie on a hook, bust open a soldier (a pretty big, very aggressive, terrestrial hermit crab), and let fly. The line spirals off the end of the spool like a spinning reel. The favorite fish of those folks is parrot fish, but they'll eat most any snapper, squirrel fish, wrasse, moray eel, grouper, triggerfish, barracuda, tarpon, grunt, angelfish, cowfish . . . most anything, but they would rather have a parrot fish and they are expert at catching that particular critter, too. A parrot fish is, next to a sheephead, the most adept of bait stealers. They are set up just like a parrot in the mouth and, if you dive and watch them, they eat like a parrot . . . nibble skillfully at little things and separate out the good part, like the bait, and let the trash (like the hook) fall. "You have to pull just before he bites" is the advice of experts like Ivan and Manny to frustrated newcomers to the sport.

Anyway, they would catch parrot fish and bring them back to the trailer and invite me over for supper on Sunday night. I was delighted to get to go, too, even though that little weekly visit cut me back to about three hours of sleep that night. They had a tiny, travel-trailer-sized propane gas stove and a tiny black-and-white television set and were very proud of both. As soon as they saw me drive up to my little cattywampus outfit in the old sticky car, they would ceremoniously come up and invite me for supper. "We will watch the television set while we cook supper," they always announced.

First, they scaled the parrot fish (very big scales), head and all. Then they gutted him, being very careful to excise the rectum without any waste. Then they would put him into their pot and parboil him (or her or them) on the stove while they washed and cut up the salad and the ingredients of the soup. They did this part of the preparation sitting on their chairs pulled up, along with mine, which I had brought from my trailer, in a semicircle around the TV, which sat on a wire-spool in the middle of the tiny living quarters of the little trailer. It was *The Ed Sullivan Show,* and they would marvel at the spectacle of the likes of Topo Gigio, the little Italian rat, various acrobats, and Shari Lewis talking lip to lip with Lamb Chop (at that, Manny would hitch at his britches and pronounce her, "A very attractive woman, no?"). I saw the Beatles for the first time with Ivan and Manny, who did not appear to understand the significance of the great event, and I am afraid I even dozed off for a few "Yeah, yeah, yeahs" myself. There was no TV on St. Martin or Saba back then, so everything on there was a big deal to those poor fellows. Now, I am going to stop right here and tell you something: I can't see the point to all this luxury. I bet you any amount of money that Ivan was just as overjoyed to get back behind his picket fence with his little family as John Lennon was to get back to the hotel with Yoko. Pure joy is about as far as you can go . . . ain't no point in over-accessorizing it.

Anyway, back to the recipe: They always made two dishes for Sunday supper. They sat there on their chairs and carefully picked all the meat off those parrot fish. They had two plastic bowls and they put the meat off the bodies of the fish into one and the skin and the meat of the heads in the other. They even separated the vertebrae (parrot fish have very big bones) and extracted the spinal nerve to put into the head bowl. They didn't waste a thing. There wasn't enough left on the bones to interest a mongoose when they got through picking. They made a salad with the meat of the body of the fish and put the head meat back in the pot with the broth, and added some onions and other things to make a soup. I am going to have to interrupt the smooth flow of this narrative again. You just think you know what's gourmet fare if you have never eaten what people like Manny and Ivan have for Sunday supper every week. The salad was variable in its content depending on availability, but onions and lime juice were always in there. Sometimes they would have some little raw green beans and usually a can of garbanzos. Any kind of fresh raw greens might go in and always plenty of pepper and salt. It really didn't make all that much difference . . . the parrot fish was the best part.

The soup from the head was the next course. Except for the fish, onions were the main thing in there. The rind of the lime that was squeezed for the salad was cut up in there, too. I think, sometimes, a red or yellow bell pepper might have been included and maybe some celery or maybe some carrots. Though the ingredients of the two dishes were similar, the results were completely different. But both of them were absolutely delicious. I always went home and slept like I had been bitten by a tsetse fly.

Now, I am from the Deep South (born and raised in a brier patch about two miles north of the Florida line). These people down here are fried fish fiends. They'll bake a flounder every now and then and grill the steaks of a big fish like a cobio, but what they really like to do is to shake the salted and peppered fillets in corn meal and fry them in deep peanut oil. If you put the fillets in, skin side down, the vaporization of the water will bubble the skin away from the meat and the fillets will turn over all by themselves when the time comes. If done right it ain't half bad, either, and the first time I went to Sunday supper, I couldn't believe what Manny and Ivan were doing. I thought that the hardworking po' fellas were doing their fish that way because they just couldn't afford any frying oil (any store-bought anything was very expensive in St. Croix). I certainly learned my lesson. They did it like that because that's the best way to do it.

Sheephead Head Soup

You need at least one sheephead head. Sheepheads are just about the equivalent of parrot fish around here. They both eat little things that they find living on rocks or pilings or boats . . . things like barnacles, little mussels, oyster spat, little shrimp, crabs, worms, and amphipods. They, like parrot fish, have strong muscles in their heads that enable them not only to bite hard, but to wiggle their jaw from side to side to separate the good from the bad. They have the most human-looking teeth of any fish and, inside their mouths, they have little nubbin teeth all over their palate which they use to grind up hard shells and fish-hooks. Sheepheads are very good fish no matter how you cook them, but like parrot fish, they have very big bones and the boneless part of the fillet winds up mighty small considering the extent of what's left. Anyone who throws away the backbone of a sheephead is extravagantly wasteful and anybody who throws away the head is crazy. Cut out the gills and simmer the whole head in salty water (I use seawater, but that depends on where you live). I like to put a lime rind in there, too, with a whole onion and some peppercorns. There is no need to try to scale the head because, unlike parrot fish, it is impossible; besides, the skin comes off very easily after the head is poached.

After you get the head simmered for about an hour, let it cool enough so you can hitch your little chrome-plated steel chair with the thin vinyl cushion right up close to the TV and you and your roommate can watch the show while you pick out the meat. You'll be astonished at what you get. The head of a fish is not actually a solid skull but many small, barely attached plates of bone separated by discrete muscles. The eyeball muscles are even easy to get out and there is a jelly around the eyeball itself that is very good. The cooking solidifies the lens of the eye until it is about like a dried lentil and too hard to eat, but the rest enhances the soup most excellently. The jaws and teeth, when cleaned, dried, and put back together, are an interesting ornament. My sister has a set on the windowsill of the pantry and even the prissiest of passersby cannot escape a double take. Family members all exclaim, "Jesus, that looks exactly like your momma after Dr. Gravely scraped off the pyorrhea."

After you get it all picked out, put the meat back in the pot with the onions (leeks will work fine), lime rinds, and whatever else you have scratched up (ain't nothing wrong with a little cauliflower and some celery, either. I like to season with red and black pepper and that hot Hungarian paprika—can't go wrong). Stew it for long enough to cook the onions down (don't hurt to fry them in a little olive oil to hurry up the process) and then dip yourself up a little bowl. You'll see. Don't eat it all, though.

Cold sheephead head soup is a marvelous thing. It jells into the most wonderful consommé. It kind of stratifies before it solidifies and the pepper settles to the bottom. If you can get it out in one piece, it is best to turn it over so you can see exactly where to cut . . . might be a scale on the bottom.

Sheepheads

The actual accepted common name is *sheepshead*, but people who live where sheepshead live call them "sheepheads." You know how your momma told you not to cross your eyes because they might stick that way? I think if you say "sheepshead" too much, you might develop a bad lisp.

Anyway, sheepheads are good-sized (two or three pounds on the average) bream-shaped saltwater fish with alternating black and white vertical stripes. Sheepheads have a mighty sheepish-looking face. They usually hang around in small groups of two or three but sometimes there will be twenty or so hiding out in a hole or under the pilings of a dock. Though they will wander along the seaside beach right in the surf looking for mole crabs and *Donax* (the genus of little bivalves that tourists call coquinas), they like to hang out around objects like stumps and rocks. They love oyster bars and will hang around a big stingaree while he is digging so as to steal a snack. I have seen sheepheads biting barnacles off big horse conchs and *Busycon* conchs. They don't work very hard at anything and are very fat . . . absolutely delicious. Sheepheads are highly prized by expert inshore fishermen like me. They would be extinct if they weren't so hard to catch.

You are really beginning to approach becoming as capable as your ignorant ancestors when you can catch a sheephead. I won't go into how hard it is to do with a hook and line. There are some people who can actually do it, but they keep their own counsel. I have caught one or two like that, but I ain't got the patience to sit there and snatch and cuss for hours and hours. I throw the cast net over them. They are very alert and fast, but if the conditions are right, they can be caught. What you have to do is catch them when the water is cloudy enough that you can barely see them and they can't see you throw. The water has to be deep, too, or they'll dart when the net hits the water and run out from under it. They dart a distance that is inverse to the depth of the water. If it is shallow, they'll run clean away; if it is medium deep, they'll probably run just outside the drop of the leads. If it is deep, they'll just give a little twitch and let the net settle, most satisfactorily, over them. Sheepheads don't act like most fish when they realize that something has got them. They don't tear around inside the net like crazy, they just bristle up and stick right where they are (black drum do that same thing. I once caught one of those, in an eight-foot net, that must have weighed thirty pounds). With that, I am going to let you in on my little secret. When the tide runs out, sheepheads congregate in deep holes and wait. If you know where the holes are and can get back in there . . . and manage not to get hung up (takes a lot of boggy research), you can hit the jackpot. Dang, I wish Ivan and Manny could come for supper.

SEA TURTLE

in which I learn my lesson
about being so presumptuous . . . well, almost

IN THE SUMMER of 1967 I was trying out a pretty little boat that I had built for this fortunate person. I put a piece of carpet on the transom so that my old ragged outboard motor wouldn't booger up the varnish and took it out on the flats to see how wonderful it was. While I was tooling around out there, I saw this dead sea turtle floating with just the ridge of his carapace above water and his head and feet hanging down like they do when they have fermented a while after being drowned in a shrimp trawl. I eased carefully up alongside him with my paddle so I wouldn't disturb any little fish that were taking refuge in his shadow before I could get a chance to examine them (and so there would be no chance to skin up the paint on old Fortunate's boat). He was sort of small for a sea turtle and had a rough shell, so I figured that he might be a hawksbill (the tortoiseshell sea turtle). I floated there alongside him for a long time looking at the little fish that were with him and trying to decide what to do. Hawksbills, never plentiful around here, were very rare by then, so I decided to ease him into the boat and take him to Gainesville to Archie Carr.* That would do two things, I figured: Contribute a specimen of a rare animal without having to kill it, and give me an excuse to go see Dr. Carr. I grabbed the turtle by the sides of his shell and slipped him carefully over the varnished gunwale of the little boat. It turned out to be the wrong thing to do.

In the first place, he was not a hawksbill sea turtle at all. He wasn't any kind of a *sea* turtle, but a common freshwater alligator snapping turtle (*Macrochelys temminckii*—perfectly described by Carr and Coleman Goin in their *Guide to the Reptiles, Amphibians and Fresh Water Fishes of Florida* as "A big, dark, long-tailed, big headed and ill natured brute of a turtle with a hard, fast strike and no color pattern") and he wasn't rare, he wasn't dead, and he wasn't even a he.

I saw evidence of the "hard fast strike" immediately, and cowered to the very stern of the boat with my feet up on the seat. She decided to go the other way and wedged herself under the front seat where she began to tear up the boat. First she bit the carefully carved stem knee into ruin, then she kicked with her feet until she busted the elegant lightweight seat loose from the clamp, clawed the varnish down to the bare wood in about fifty places, and bit

---

*Dr. Archie Carr of the University of Florida in Gainesville was the sea turtle man of the world. Not only was he an effective researcher and powerful teacher, he was the most eloquent writer. If you have never read *The Windward Road* and *So Excellent a Fishe* you are in for a treat.

my tiny precious Danforth anchor so pigeon-toed that the shank could no longer pass between the flukes and the galvanize was popped off in about five places. I tried to rake her out from under the seat with my carefully scraped and treasured quarter-sawn (by hand) ash paddle and she, with a flip of her big, ugly head, bit it half in two. I would have shot her at that juncture if I could have gotten to my tackle box, but she beat me to it. I wish I had it back.

Years before, when I was working on construction jobs to get through college and support the boatbuilding business, I got laid off for about a long, miserable, rainy week during Christmas vacation. I spent the whole time building this tiny, elaborate wood tackle box. All the compartments had little sliding wood covers, and the miniature dovetailed trays fit together so perfectly that you could turn it upside down and not a single split shot, swivel, or narrow hook would get out of place. I was going to send it to my father for a Christmas present, but couldn't bring myself to part with it right then. Well, part with it I did, that day. That damned turtle bit it into smithereens in just one snap. All that was left were splinters, little tiny rectangular compartment lids, a snarl of chewed up leaderwire, ruined plugs, and bent hooks. I saw my pistol only as a flash as it flipped over the side.

After eating the front of the boat up, she busted her way out from under the seat and headed aft. I went over the stern taking the broken-off tiller of the outboard with me where it was hung up in the britches leg of my shorts. She started working on the stern immediately. I couldn't see exactly what she was doing, but the sound was terrible and I recognized parts of the boat and pieces of my gear that were thrown in the water with me. I noticed the drain plug when it went "ploop" right beside my ear. By the time I could gnaw and rip the cheap (but tough) seventy percent polyester sleeve off my T-shirt to stuff into the hole (I started to stick my finger in there, like the little Dutch boy, temporarily, while I worked on the shirt, but thought better of it), the boat was very low in the water. While I was concentrating, the turtle slipped over the side and disappeared.

In a way, it was a good thing and in another, it wasn't. The boat was so low in the water that I couldn't get in without risk of submerging the outboard motor. Without it or the paddle, I would be in a famous fix, not up just a little polluted creek but two miles out there on the flats. So, I started frantically to dip water with my hands. I couldn't even hang on to the boat while I was doing this because, with the motor on there, it was so tippy. I had to keep wiggling my twinkle-toed feet enticingly the whole time. You know, unlike alligators and snakes, turtles do most of their feeding underwater. I hurried up, the best I could, but it was a long, long time before I could get back in the boat. Then I had to turn the gas tank over and let the water out from under the gas into the engine shroud to avoid contaminating the inside of the boat or the rest of the world. After that jackleg decantation, I had to improvise a throttle, tiller handle, and choke knob. By the time I finally got back to the boat ramp holding the fuel hose onto the little titty with my cramped left hand and steering and throttling with the high-speed knob with my right, it was dark thirty—and I (reeking of gasoline) still had to drive eighty miles to get home.

Something good did come out of this anyway. I couldn't deliver that boat to old Fortunate because I had to paint the inside to hide the repairs and he had particularly specified that it be varnished. I had to build him another one. I still have the old turtle boat.

COBIO

*in which I save my children from starvation
but almost freeze to death in the process*

THOUGH I AM not a big-deal sports fisherman like those who
will go out in the big water and sit backward in the smoke
and troll for game fish all day long, I have caught quite a few very
big fish just messing around with my little boat trying to catch a
little something to eat. One of the most memorable was a giant
cobia (called "cobio" around here—"ling" some places) I caught
a long time ago out on the flats east of St. Marks in Apalachee
Bay off the Big Bend of Florida.

I remember that it was in the early spring, pine pollen time. I
was doing a little subsistence farming back then and I had just
finished planting corn. I had nursed along my new potatoes extra
early and we had already felt around under the ground and fon-
dled out a little taste and all of us (the boys were little back then)
had wished for a fish to go with them. I don't know about you,

but to us, big-dice new potatoes scrubbed so the skin can stay on and just boiled up in the pot and daubed with plenty of butter (that's butter, not oleo) just cry out for a piece of fish to keep them company on the plate. We vowed to leave those potato (red Pontiac) bushes alone until we could do it right.

This was before 1970—back when I was still trying to build plywood boats and I had the old turtle boat. I don't even remember what kind of outboard I had on there at that time, but I know it was a piece of junk . . . might have been a Scott Attwater ("Afraidawater" to some). Might have been an old pump-primer Johnson five that I had for a while . . . one of those that had two separate carburetors: a tiny venturi kind of like a model airplane for idling and a regular float-bowl style one for running . . . both apt to dribble gas at any time. It certainly wasn't a Martin, which I always wished I had. I kept one serviced for a man and it was a good motor, but that ain't got nothing to do with this cobio business.

I knew it was too early for the water to have warmed up for the speckled trout to be doing anything. Them and the reds would probably still be up in the rivers with a hundred jillion crackers anchored as close together around the hole (when it gets cold, fish from the flats seek deep water, such as limesinks in rivers, and catching them is like fishing in a barrel) as the patrons at a chicken fight.

I must digress a little right here and explain about crackers. They were named that back in the days when Georgia and Florida teamsters drove big teams of oxen or mules hauling logs and other freight over the awful roads they had back then. They cracked long bullwhips to give the poor animals an incentive to continue.

The ox teams are gone and the crackers have degenerated into being what are commonly called "rednecks," which was the word for the poor old white dirt farmers of this region whose necks got red from bending over the hoe all day long in the hot sun. Though the original meanings have been forgotten by most, both names continue to hang on to designate a class of Southerner, the men of whom drive pickup trucks and spit out the window. You know, there are various degrees of Southerners. I ain't going to go all into it, but we are easily disturbed by being called out of our name. The only corollary I can think of to the north is how y'all have all kinds of people who hang on to the ways of their ancestral country of origin. When I was in the Navy I learned a bunch of names for various kinds of Yankees, and it didn't do to get them confused, either. Like everybody in Minnesota ain't a Norwegian bachelor farmer, down here, we ain't all rednecks . . . for instance, some of us are black.

Dang. All them aside, since I ain't crazy about indiscriminate socializing around a hole in the river with no chew-tobacco-crackers, I decided to take my chances out on the flats. It was a nice day . . . sort of breezy out of the east in the morning, but it soon calmed completely off. I knew the no-see-ums were eating those speck fishermen up back there, but it was so tranquil out on flats that I began to imagine that I was not in an outboard motor powered boat at all and that my Zebco was not on my pole and my hook was a tiny stingaree spine lashed to a piece of shell by a strand of *Yucca filamentosa*. I readied myself.

There was nothing biting down there at all. The fish wouldn't even steal my bait (cut-up pinfish, *Lagodon rhomboides*, good to eat, too, as is all good bait—my grandmother used to eat all the bait up before we were through fishing). I could see some little wrasses and other grass dwellers swimming around, but there were no black rock bass (sea bass) or any grunts (pigfish) or any other of the usual denizens of the turtle grass (*Thalassia* in the gulf, equivalent to the also diminishing *Zostera* of the Atlantic flats— God help us). What I had hoped would happen was that the wonderful spring pompano would decide to cruise by, but they didn't. Since the dream was fading, I was just about to pull up and leave to go back to Georgia in time to shoot a few squirrels—which, don't let the degenerate nature of your dependence on store-bought goods fool you: Squirrels, either boiled, fried, baked, grilled, or barbecued, beat hell out of a lot of manufactured things. I am apt to nail them any chance I get, but the one that I remember best was a squirrel who missed stays crossing the road on a high wire and fell onto my neck while I was driving down the street in my old convertible Cadillac. Before the squirrel could figure out what to do, I had him wrapped up in a rag and stuffed into the glove box so I could deal with him later. When I got home and inspected him, though, I saw that he was so big-codded that I knew he would be rank. I am an epicure, so I turned him loose.

Wandering back to the fish story, here I was, at anchor, dreaming, out there on the flats, in my unpaid-for skiff, hoping to catch a fish. And I did. I had decided to try one more spot and I had found a little hill of rocks like are so common on the flats of the "big bend" and was able to catch one or two little black rock bass. What I was hoping for was a sheephead, which, as far as I know, are just about the only inshore fish unaffected by the very low water temperature (for this region) caused not only by the water being so thin that the cold nights can nip it all the way to the bottom, but also by the cooling effect of evaporation when the dry-northers blow. There weren't any sheepheads on that rock pile, though, and I was just about to pull up and go home after I caught one or two more of the bass—just enough for a little taste—when something grabbed one of the little fish that I was pulling in. I didn't know what it was at first, but it stripped line off my Zebco like it was going to get it all . . . then it stopped and I thought for sure it was a stingaree, which will act like that. Then I saw an enormous fish swim right under the boat where he stopped. I could barely see him under there, but I knew immediately what he was.

I think I ought to tell you about the little hills of rocks like the one where I was. Most of them are limestone. All the coast of the big bend is limestone, kind of like the Bahamas. There is a little more sand on top of it here, but it ain't very deep and the limestone often pokes through. It makes for dangerous navigation, which is a good thing—sort of helps to keep thoughtless people in their place. Sometimes in a dry fall when the rivers run so slow that they can't carry much agricultural or urban runoff, the water clears up almost like the Bahama banks or the Caribbean or the Keys before all that sugarcane. We love to snorkel on the flats when that happens.

One time, when it was like that and our boys were little, we went to one of the rock outcroppings between the St. Marks and Aucilla rivers. The water wasn't but about eighteen inches deep, but it was as clear as glass and we swam around with the warm sun on our backs for hours looking at pinfish, wrasses, scallops, shrimp, burrowing anemones, and all sorts of denizens. Finally, one of our boys found a piece of chipped flint, then another and then another. There were a bunch of them—rejects. That outcropping of limestone had encapsulated nodules of flint and the wild people had gone out there and knocked off what they needed.

Anyway, cobio love to hang around any kind of object in the water. When they are migrating in the spring they'll stop off at channel markers, moored boats, rock piles, pilings, anything, even tiny little things like crab trap buoys. One of my uncles caught one that was circling a bloated-up dead goat. They don't mind shallow water, either. I have even seen them circling a crab trap that was sticking out of the water. Cobio are very decisive fish. If they don't want to eat, you can throw all kinds of delicacies right under their noses and they'll just circle past and wave their tails at it. But if they are in the mood, most any kind of live sea creature, even a full-grown blue crab or a puff fish, is snapped up with no ceremony.

This one particular cobio had swum over to see what was what with that object floating dreamily beside the rock pile, and had found a little snack trying to get away from a little string in its mouth. My line wasn't but about six-pound test, or maybe even four—like I said, I ain't a major league sportsman and you can catch a lot more eating-sized fish on light line than you can with big game stuff. I tried to gingerly lead that big fish out from under the boat so I could maybe hook him with the gaff. He was so big (he looked to be about my size) that I was a little afraid to gaff him and sure didn't want to put him in the boat too green to handle, so I really didn't know what the hell to do. I did succeed in pulling him around so that his head was sticking out from under the side, but I couldn't hold him without straightening out my little hook, and he went right back in the shade. I sat there for a long time trying to think of something to do. Finally I decided to see if he would let me pull anchor and slowly ease over closer to the bank where it was shallow enough that I could get out after the gaff was in him. But as soon as I pulled the boat a little bit toward the anchor, he swam off slowly, taking line off the reel. Holding the rod in one hand as he stripped off the little bit of line a Zebco will hold, I pulled the anchor with the other hand and my teeth (pull an arm's length, bite the bight, pull another, bite, and pull again—I knew a one-armed grouper fisherman who handlined like that all his life). I was scrambling back to the engine to see if maybe I could get started before all the line was gone when he quit running again and pretty soon, here he came back under the boat. As soon as he had settled down and I had my line back, I began to gently scull the boat toward the faraway shore. He stayed with me for a little while but then he took off again. It was the same as before. He ran slowly out about fifty yards and then turned around and came back.

This thing could get boring if I was to tell it blow by blow, so I'll just hit the high points from now on. It turned out that he would only stay with the boat if I stayed near the rock pile. If I tried to go toward the shore, just as soon as he realized that he wasn't right where he wanted to be, he would swim off. If I had succeeded in moving very much, he would go back to the rock pile instead of the boat and I was afraid he would cut my line on some barnacles or oysters so I tried my best to do what he wanted me to do which was to stay close to the rocks so he would feel comfortable. I was afraid to anchor again, not only because I was worried that it might spook him for good, but sometimes he would make four or five circles around the boat just to check out his territory, I guess, and I knew he would wrap up with the anchor line, so I had to hold the boat against the tide (still not a breath of wind) by sculling all afternoon while I tried to get up the nerve to gaff him. I wished I'd had my little mullet harpoon. You know, a gaff hook on a pole puts you and the fish together in pretty rigid way and a big fish on a short gaff will hurt you. A harpoon connects you and the fish with a stout line and that not only lets him stay far enough away that he can't actually hit you, but doesn't try to snatch and twist your arm out of joint quite so bad. If I'd had my harpoon I would have been home with him by then. Guess what's under the seats of my boat along with my oars right now?

Finally it got so late that I knew it would be dark by the time I could get back to the boat ramp so I decided to lead him out and see if I could, maybe, snatch-hook him under the jaw with a bigger hook from my tackle box and a short section of quarter-inch braided nylon line that I had. I knew he would probably pull my arm out of joint (he was a very big fish) and put a rope burn on me that would stay for weeks, but I couldn't think of anything else, so I opened up the tackle box to get the hook; there I spied my pistol. "Dammit," I wailed, "why didn't I think of that a long time ago?"

It was an old, rusty, Browning-style (Fabrique National, Belgium) 9mm war pistol that my wife's uncle Dave had liberated during WWII. I could never hit a thing with it, but it was so rusty and useless that I kept it in my tackle box sort of like ballast. The old thing had a clip that held about umpteen shells and they were solid-nosed and I hoped that they would penetrate enough water that I could do enough damage so he would give out before my line did. I urged him out from under the boat again. It took a few tries before I could get his head up shallow enough that I thought the puny pistol bullet might be able to reach something vital.

I hate to stop right here and let this out, but members of my family have shot quite a few fish. My grandmother was the worst of us about it. Every spring, when the bass (largemouth bass— freshwater fish) went on the bed in the shallow water of the fringes of our old, big, swampy pond, she would set up her tripod rig and wade out and climb up before day and as soon as she could see, she would nail one really big female bass with her .25/35, which all those who do that know is the best penetrator of water. They say it's because it has such a long skinny bullet. I am way off the track now, but I guess I'll just have to tell this story. After the men all came home from WWII, one of my uncles had a Japanese war rifle that he had picked up. I think it was 6.5mm, but whatever it was, it had a very long, skinny bullet and everybody wanted to know how it would work for shooting fish, so when the spring of '46 came, they set up the tripod and this uncle climbed up to the seat before day and shot a big bass with the war rifle. He was set up kind of awkward and the tripod was sort of inexpertly arranged and he hit the water about the same time as the bullet (is that proof of some law of physics?). My grandmother said she didn't care if that thing would shoot through three feet of water, she was going to stay with her .25/35. Which I still have.

And which I wished for when I pulled that big cobio out from under the boat for the last time. I aimed that pooty pistol as carefully as I could in the dusk-dark . . . just behind the gills where the spine goes into the skull and, trying as hard as I could not to flinch, squeezed the rusty trigger. Blap-blap-blap-blappety-blap-blap . . . That thing shot like a machine gun so many times that I thought it must be manufacturing shells somehow. It didn't seem like it would ever stop, and after it finally did, water fell down out of the sky for about ten minutes. I found out what the trouble was later. The firing pin was so rusty that it had stuck in the hole and every time the slide cycled and the shell hit bottom, it hit the primer and so on. I had to sit down and calm myself after all that.

When I finally got straight, I looked over the side and there was my fish lying on the bottom in about ten feet of water. I could see a little blood diffusing out of one hole right where I had aimed. Now what? When I pulled on the line, I found that it was still hooked up to him and I tried to lift him up from the bottom, but he was so heavy that, though I could raise his head a little bit, I knew I would never pull him up high enough to reach, so I started trying to lash the gaff to an oar (while sculling and tending the rod, too). Finally I realized that it was soon going to be so dark that I wouldn't be able to see him down there anymore and he and all this fooling around would be wasted . . . besides, it was getting cold, so I did what I had to do. Man, that water was cold. I like to have froze to death before I finally got back to the ramp.

I felt like some kind of animal as I finally dragged in with my prey and all the other little animals came to sniff at what I had brought them. We cut that big fish into steaks and, even though it was late and a school night, grilled some on a bed of coals out in the yard—pot of new potatoes steaming to the side, plate of butter gathering ashes. He was delicious, too, bless his soul. I was certainly sorry when I went to the freezer and found that those big steaks had been eaten up, but by then, there were plenty of lesser fish out on the flats.

THE GIANT CATFISH OF MOBILE

in which I meet an astonishing transvestite . . .
and cook breakfast

I USED TO WORK on tugboats in order to make enough money
to stay in the boatbuilding business. It worked out pretty good.
I would tug for twenty days and then had ten days off to build on
the boat. I used to cheat a little and figure out what I was going
to do on the boat while I was on the tug. I carved half models and
drew plans, developed the panels for V-bottomed plywood boats,
and even did my lofting out on the barge so I could carry the
patterns for the molds home folded up in my suitcase.

The tugboat I mostly worked on was a captive deal. I could
quit any time I wanted to and come back and get on when I got
ready. They had a terrible run. There was this one little Gulf Coast
town where there was a tradition of small, locally owned, seagoing
tugs that contracted to haul petroleum barges across the Gulf from
the giant refineries in Mississippi Sound, Louisiana, and Texas to

the power plants and tank farms down on the Florida peninsula. These little boats (all under ninety feet) ran all the time, and were so trustworthy that they just about had a monopoly on the petroleum contracts beyond the eastern terminus of the Gulf Intracoastal Waterway at Dog Island. Because the boats were so little and diligent, the captains had a hard scrabble to try to keep a crew on there during the winter, particularly after it got to where folks didn't have to work to eat. Though it is not legendary for roughness like, say, Cape Horn, the shallow Gulf of Mexico is a rough little piece of water some of the time. I can remember some trips when we were trying to come back from some place like Crystal River with two empty barges on the towline in a norther when we hammered on the same spot for forty-eight hours. When I got to where I needed a little cash, all I would have to do was show up, with my suitcase and a big grin, about Christmastime. I know how to cook, splice big lines and wires, and fix junk machinery. I advise anybody who wants an easy job on a tugboat to learn to do those things. If you can do that, you always got a ticket to ride—at least in a non-union situation in the wintertime among desperate people.

This story ain't got nothing to do with all that, though. I was cooking on there one time about 1971 when we had to go in for a crankshaft job. Most of those little old boats had two engines. This one had sixteen-cylinder 99 Caterpillars but some of the boats ran GM, EMD (Electro Motive Division of General Motors, still two cycle) railroad locomotive engines, and quite a few still had the old Atlas or Enterprise heavy-duty, direct reversible (that's where you had to shut the engine down, rotate the camshaft drive gear a little bit, and crank it back up running backward to get reverse) engines. The engineers on those boats could do most any kind of overhaul work on one engine while the other was running so we didn't have to stop and hurt our reputation. We replaced pistons, liners, and connecting rod bearings, did cylinder head jobs, turbocharger bearings, rebuilt and calibrated injector pumps and injectors, rodded out oil coolers, fixed pumps, generators, all kinds of junk—all that at sea—rocking and rolling down in the unbelievable din and heat of the engine room, dancing cheek to cheek with each other and the two engines, one scattered and sliding all over the place and the other one thundering loud and scorching hot. We did that so we could keep running, which was the only way a small operation could beat out the fierce competition from Louisiana. We could do all that at sea, but we had to go to the hill to take the top of an engine off the base to change out a crankshaft and main bearings. We called ahead to the yard, though, and had everything set up so we wouldn't cool off too much while we were out of fix.

I was having a little trouble with this old second engineer on there. He didn't like me and I didn't like him. Though it was against the rules to let personal differences interfere with the work of the vessel, we both pushed it pretty good. Every morning, I would get up about four o'clock and cook breakfast for six men (three at one sitting, captain, engineer, deckhand, and then they would relieve the other three and I would feed them). It was a ritual on there that they had the same thing for breakfast every morning. I would put two strips of bacon for each man in the pan and, while those were trying out, I would make the biscuits in an iron frying pan . . . seven biscuits . . . six catheads around the rim and one hexagon in the middle . . . buttermilk biscuits, shortened with bacon grease. After I had put the frying pan in the oven and put on a pot of grits, the bacon would have shrunk up enough so I could put in the sausages. Those and the eggs were the only variable allowed in the breakfast ritual. The sausages could be either link style or patty style and the eggs were cooked to order as the men came and got their coffee and sat down. I always thought it was a fairly good breakfast back before they discovered cholesterol. It was also a pretty nice sociable occasion until this fool got the ass.

At first he started complaining that I was overcooking the bacon. I even tried to take his two strips out a little early, but then he whined, "This bacon done got cold. This must be left over from yestiddy." Then, "These is some soupy damn grits. You cain't cook a goddamn biscuit neither." The eggs were never right. "This what you call over easy? These damn eggs is plum leathery." He would eat it all, though, and wipe up the grease out of his plate with his last biscuit. I put up with all that complaining until we got tied up beside the dry dock for the crankshaft job on the port engine. One morning, since nobody was on watch, we were all crowded in the galley eating breakfast and he announced, "I cain't eat this. This ain't fit for a dog." With that, I stomped over there and snatched his breakfast out from under his big red nose and, with one fluid motion, opened the starboard side galley door and flung the complete contents of his plate up against the side of the rusty floating dry dock, where they slid down into the nasty water of the Alabama River. The yard men were already welding on another old junk boat in the dry dock, and in that ghastly flicker, I saw the sausages, eggs, and the palette of grits slide out of sight beneath the slick from the bacon grease and the fuel and oil that

is always around places like that. The two biscuits were left floating in the scum.

After I got through washing the dishes and pots and pans (and
listening to a few impotent threats), I went out on deck to see the
morning. I noticed that there was only one biscuit floating in the
bacon grease. I wondered about that. I was thinking to myself,
"Theoretically, identical biscuits should do the same thing under
identical conditions," when I saw this enormous pair of pale gray
lips rise up, solemnly, under the remaining biscuit. There was a
long, slow, deliberate, loud suction noise and the biscuit gradually
began to spin in a counterclockwise direction. A vortex slowly
formed and the biscuit was sucked down into those lips. I was
mesmerized.

I knew where two more biscuits were.* Our "old captain" (we
had two captains on at the time, the other one was the "little
captain") didn't have any teeth. Oh, he had this set of cheap chop-
pers that were used only for display, but he couldn't eat with them.

---

*I know damned well that there will be some biscuit-counting nitpickers
among you gracious readers, so I'll explain the situation so you can rest easy. On
some crews there were people who, like me, did not eat biscuits. The reason I
don't eat them is that I believe the invention of the biscuit heralds the day of the
beginning of the decline of mankind into the wretched state we are in now. A
biscuit is an abstraction, sort of like car insurance. Civilization is an abstraction,
sort of like cars. On this crew, Junior (the other captain) did not eat biscuits,
either. He didn't even eat breakfast. He always came down in the middle of the
night (made his engineer steer) and ate up all the leftovers from supper. He could
eat half a gallon of black-eyed peas and two ham hocks . . . bones and all. When
I had to cook for other crews in other biscuit situations, I made eight biscuits in
the pan and the middle one turned out to be octagonal. . . . So there, damn your
eyes.

Us cooks always saved out two of the biscuits (one of the catheads and the hexagon) so he could mash them up in his bowl with his fork and some buttermilk. Since he had his teeth in this morning so he could effectively negotiate with the dignitaries of the crankshaft job, I decided to flip one of his biscuits over the side to see if I couldn't get a better look at those toilet-seat-sized lips. It worked real good. Not only did I see the lips, but clotted, slimy whiskers, as fat around as somebody's fingers, two opaque, milky-blind eyes, and a hint of the body of an enormous catfish. I dashed for the captain's last biscuit and my handline.

To make a long story short, hooking him was easy but I couldn't stop him from going back under the dry dock and cutting me off. I tried again, but when I saw my hook stuck in his lip and scars from other hooks, I felt bad and quit trying to catch him. One old man who was trying to braze up some of the worst of the notches in the propeller of the boat on the dry dock with a huge acetylene torch said that catfish had been living under that dry dock for all the thirty years he had been working there and that nobody could catch him. "Too much steel on the bottom, besides, he is big enough to eat a grown man." "That a fact?" chirped me.

It was boring on the boat in the shipyard. I wandered around all through the old place looking at all the artifacts left over from when they used to work on wood boats (there was a gigantic shipsaw all grown up in the bushes for one thing) and messed around in the river with the little aluminum skiff we kept on the roof, and even went up to the causeway one night with the deckhand to this little bar. There, the deckhand met an amazingly extroverted woman who was so charming that he decided to go to her house as a guest. After they drove off through the tunnel to Mobile in her Mustang, I trudged it on back to the boat. About three o'clock in the morning, I heard somebody stomping onto the eerily quiet boat and went to see. There was the deckhand washing up for bed. "What happened to your woman?" I asked. "That wasn't no goddamn woman," he replied, disgustedly. "Had to leave my goddamn shoes and my money," he lamented. "You don't never want to walk home through no goddamn tunnel without no shoes," he concluded.

Fortunately, I didn't have to do that. I was able to catch the bus right out there on the causeway when I got tired of all that and walked off the job one more time.

KING TUT

*in which I prove the disclaimer that none
of these stories could possibly be true*

ALITTLE AFTER THAT biscuit-catfish incident—maybe 1979—
the tug was waiting our turn to lock out of the Mississippi
River going west when I read in the newspaper that King Tut with
all his raiments and accoutrements was on display across the river
at the Sugar Bowl. I could see right where he was from where we
were tied up to some bushes. They were having some kind of
trouble with the lock and we had been tied up to the same bushes
for so long that the paperboy had put us on his route and we had
started running a trot line alongside the barges. One night, I was
up in the wheelhouse trying to get away from the company when
I heard the lock talking on the radio. There were so many boats
tied up along the river that there were some thirty lockings ahead
of us. I had plenty of time to swim the river and go see King Tut.

I took off all my clothes and shoes, put them into a white

plastic bucket, clenched a sock with my collection of Susan B. Anthony dollars in my teeth, and climbed down the tires into the river. Pushing my white bucket in front of me, I started swimming. I have had a little experience with that old swift river and ain't stupid, so I didn't delude myself that I could swim straight across to the dome. I figured I would need a little hiding place to put on my clothes anyway, so some less exposed downriver landing would be just fine. I was in no hurry to get back to the boat, so I planned to pull out of the river someplace down by the Huey P. Long bridge, wipe off a little bit with my rag, put on my clothes and shoes, and stroll back to the dome. I got messed up, though.

Just about the time I got to the middle of the river and began to adjust my estimate of a landing site because I was making such good time, a damned tanker (EXXON PASCAGOULA . . . MONROVIA, LIBERIA) that had been anchored upriver of us, waiting to get to the dock, decided that it was time to go, hauled anchor, swung broadside the river, and came down on me. I had to skee-daddle sideways like a crab to get out of the way. While I was trying to make up my mind if I wanted to swim downriver, contrary to my notions, around the stern or try upriver around the bow, we drifted so far that I wound up way the hell-and-gone down below the Tenneco refinery at Chalmette. The bank was steep and rooty and when I finally got myself hauled out, I was worn out from the decision-making process and didn't have my plastic bucket anymore.

I started searching in the dark through the horrendous mess of trash along the bank for something to wear. Finally, I settled on a plastic shower curtain, which I identified by feeling the snap-on rings. I was able to use these rings, cleverly, to attach the shower curtain around me sort of like a toga. I figured, once I got up to the light and managed to scrape some of the mud off me, I wouldn't look too peculiar for New Orleans where people are used to a little peculiarity. I still had my Susans. I would just trot up the riverbank to the phone booth, just outside the refinery gate, call a cab, and go see King Tut.

I found a little, more or less clear water puddled in the asphalt of the road and splashed around in it like a bird until I couldn't feel too much grit anywhere. Then I started moseying back to town. I thought I cut a pretty fine figure in my outfit, swinging my sock full of dollars as I strutted up the road. My notions were reinforced when a car came up from behind me and blew the horn in appreciation as it passed. "Good old New Orleans," I said to myself, "what a fine place." After two or three other cars had admired me that same way, some of the occupants shouting glee-fully in appreciation, I decided I was so attractive that maybe I could stick out my thumb and eliminate the phone booth–taxicab step altogether.

It worked like a charm. A car full of happy people stopped to pick me up right away. Only after the inside lights of the car came on when the door opened did I notice that my shower curtain was one of those transparent jobs. Like I said, people in New Orleans are used to things like that. Lucky for me, they were on their way to see King Tut, too.

THE SLAVE'S RECIPE

*in which I do a little more tugging, get involved in a
criminal conspiracy, and get locked up for murder . . .
and learn a new recipe . . . and satisfy a lifelong
curiosity . . . a long story*

I HAVE A RECIPE for peach cobbler that a man from Estiffanulga
gave me about 1982. He was a slave. It wasn't 1860 or anything and the man wasn't even black, but he was a sure-enough
slave. I met him while the little tug I was working on was towing
barges of gasoline and fuel oil out of the huge refinery at Pascagoula in Mississippi Sound. We towed two barges through the
Alabama WPA ditch and the Wimico wiggles down the Jackson
River to its confluence with the mighty Apalachicola. When we
got there, we met the *Roulette,* a homemade paddle-wheel pushboat that could sometimes, eventually, push one of our barges all
the way up through the locks into Lake Seminole and on up the
Chattahoochee as far as Columbus, Georgia. We would tow the
other barge across the gulf and then up the pretty little Withla-

coochee River to the tank farm in Yankeetown between Cedar Key and Crystal River.

Roulette was an unusual boat, made by a mean old man specially to navigate the powerful and crooked Apalachicola. It was just a low, steel flatboat covered by a screen porch. There was a little shaky wheelhouse on the tin roof of the porch so the wheel man could see over the barge and an old wore-out EMD railroad locomotive engine sitting naked, on deck, right in the middle, that drove the reduction gears for the two side wheels through two enormous greasy roller-chains running off each end of a semi-truck rear axle. That axle was the key to the whole thing. The boat was steered (powerfully, I'll give him that) by working the air brakes on each end of the axle, first one side and then the other, with little rocker valves located all over the boat. There was even one steering valve beside the rusty, dangerous-looking, L.P. gas stove up under the wheelhouse so the old man who was captain, owner, and inventor of the thing could steer while he was cooking his dinner. He was so mean that most of the time he couldn't get anybody to stay on there with him to cook, make up barges, pour oil in the old engine, grease the chains, change the carbons in the searchlight, and fix the roof and screen wire, but toward the last, he had this man from Estiffanulga working as a slave on there.

This was back before insurance companies outlawed towing on the short line in inshore waters. Short tow is the cheapest and easiest way to handle a barge. You ain't always breaking all those cables and knocking all those big scabs of rust off the boat and the barge trying to make up to the stern to push. The boat can run a real short crew because all they had to do to work the barge was to take in or let out on the towline to suit the conditions of the sea or the river. Some inshore boats ran, at least some of the time, with only two men . . . one in the wheelhouse and one to work the engines and barges, cook, and catch a little snooze when he could before his turn in the wheelhouse. Even some little sea-going tugs like us had to do that when it was too cold and rough to attract a crew, but it was tough. Towing on the short line in narrow and shallow water is dangerous. Lots of tugs were run over or tripped upside down and towed under by the barges after they messed up and ran aground right there in front of the tow. Though the few pushboats, like *Roulette* (there never was another one of those), that worked the Apalachicola River had to make up astern of the barge and push because the river is so swift and tricky that running aground is the usual business, they could get by with short crews since they could push up and take a nap any time they wanted to and only had to work the barge once per trip. Which, that business was a little tricky in this situation.

As soon as we got a lull in the barge-transferring operation with the *Roulette,* the slave would swarm on board of our boat to swap porno magazines. Deckhands get tired of looking at the same old naked gals all the time. I guess that's a pretty good rule about relationships with women in general, even real ones. If you don't love them, before long, you get tired of looking at them even when they are naked. There wasn't much opportunity for conver-sation during the normal barge transfer. We would idle as slowly upstream as we could and still stay between the banks with both barges (sometimes three) on the short line while the *Roulette* tried to catch up and make up to the after barge . . . sort of like the copulation attempts of a string of ducks. As soon as he got the wires over the bits, the enslaved deckhand would run up the barges, monkeying from one to the other on the intermediate tow-lines and their wire bridles and come on us, hand over hand down the hawser like an orangutan with his magazines clenched in his teeth. While all these acrobatics were going on, the *Roulette*'s captain screamed and hollered back there about how he wanted to get tightened up to his tow and turned loose. Once or twice, the deckhand had to swim back and got his new sweethearts wet when the old man got so mad he boiled out of his wheelhouse onto the barge and himself threw off the intermediate towline between the two barges. Once the slave traded a magazine whose theme was devoted to very buxom (some could even be called fat) redheaded naked ladies with freckles and I was able to satisfy a curiosity that I have had since childhood.

One trip, when the river was low, we had to tie up to the *Roulette* long enough to visit a little. The reason that happened was because when it got dry in the fall, there wasn't enough water for a full barge to go all the way to Columbus even with that old wigglesome *Roulette* hunting the deep water. We would tie up alongside and pump half (or whatever the old turd thought he could handle) the gasoline out of one of our barges into the empty one that they had brought back. It usually took about four or five hours. The slave deckhand from the other boat would stay in our galley and eat up the leftovers, drink coffee, and try to read all the porno magazines (hundreds . . . some from back in the forties . . . ghastly stuff) that were stored under the galley seats while he gossiped with the cook—me (I alternated between cooking, decking, engineering, and in the wheelhouse depending on the season and how pissed off they were about the last time I quit). He told me his story and gave me the recipe that I cooked up for dessert that night and made a big hit with our gourmet crew.

He got to be a slave because he had run off from the state mental hospital and the word was out. That hundred or so miles on the river below the Jim Woodruff dam is just like one small town. All he would have had to do would have been to stop hiding in the swamp long enough for some sister's brother to catch a little glimpse and it would be back to Chattahoochee for him. The reason he got committed was that he had a certain attractiveness and willingness to fornicate frequently around the neighborhood. Then he would slap his thigh, laugh loudly about it, and defend himself capably when confronted by the family of the willing girl. He had simply messed with the wrong people and got into a situation of local legal manipulation that was beyond him. Bad as it was, it wasn't as bad as it could have been. Some of these old daddies will shoot a man for that. I know it may sound callous and opinion has no place in a story like this, but it might not be such a bad thing. Some girls go through a little spell where they don't seem to be able to use their own good sense and are liable to get pregnant before they are ready. If a man has to think about old daddy (or old granddaddy) and that thirty-thirty, he might pay a little more attention to what he is doing. Wouldn't be so many women who can't take good care of their children and maybe not so many people in places like Chattahoochee—like this man. He wasn't a bad person, just a reckless young fool. All he needed was something to make him think—like he had now.

As a fugitive from the mental hospital, he was hanging around the empty barge we left tied to the black gum (*Nyssa aquatica* . . . "tupelo" to real native Floridians) trees where the *Roulette* came to swap and he followed the pushboat upriver. At that time, the old captain was working the boat all by his mean-assed self and he had to tie up to the bushes every night to eat his supper and take his little nap. His evening ritual was that he would steer with his air-valve by the stove while he cooked supper to get as many miles as he could in the few days when the dam's electricity gates were open and the river was navigable. The poor hard-bitten, hungry fugitive ran through the bushes (*strolled* would be a more appropriate word; old *Roulette* wasn't no real bank washer) and smelled the cooking. After the old man pushed up for the night, the escapee slipped on board and ate up the scraps and left a few little coon turds around the deck so the old man would misblame the theft.

Before long he caught the man coming for his supper and blackmailed him into being a non-paid hand. With two people running the boat, watch and watch, the old *Roulette* managed to run twenty-four hours a day during the short times that the river was navigable, and things worked pretty good for everybody but the slave. I would have busybodied in and done something about it if I had thought it was the right thing to do, but the state hospital wasn't near as nice a place as the *Roulette*. Shoot, in those days, it wasn't even as good as Tate's Hell swamp, and I'm not so sure it's any better now.

Finally, we rusted out so bad that the company had to put our old boat in dry dock over in Mobile to half-sole the bottom one more time. What we had been doing was driving wood stobs in the rusty holes. When the old (just about in as bad shape as our boat) floating dry dock they had in Mobile finally got enough water pumped out so the old boat's bottom was visible, all those stobs sticking out of all that rust put me in mind of some old World War Two mine that you used to see in the movies. We stayed in the dry dock for a long time. The crew hung around in the galley all the time and got on my nerves and I had to take a plate once or twice. (It was a tradition on there that if a man complained about the food, the cook could snatch up his plate and substitute a paper plate, a can of Vienna sausages, and a stalk of old roachy saltines.) I went to town a couple of times and I walked up and down the riverbank, but I soon got tired of all the nastiness of Mobile and took my sock full of change and caught the bus back home.

I have been doing things like that off and on for most of my life. I worked on that same old boat a bunch of separate times for many years. I don't remember exactly what I did after I quit while they were in dry dock in Mobile. I think I drove the bus for the senior citizen's center for the summer and worked on the boat in the shop (I always have a boat in my shop, no matter what) in my off time. Anyway, when the winter came, I figured the old tug would finally be back on the job and shorthanded because of the mean conditions of the Yankeetown run when it was cold and rough. I sort of got along with the old captain who had been on there ever since the boat had been built in 1948, and even though he would get pretty pissed when I walked off, he would put me back on if I showed up grinning . . . in January. He was kind of comical about it. He would shuffle around and around in the bedroom slippers he wore all the time to try to stave off his terrible gout and work his false teeth first one cockeyed way and then the other. Finally, after he had jammed his hands down in all his pockets and snatched them back out again like he had felt something hot down in there, he would stammer his same old speech about how he ought to be ashamed of himself for encouraging sorriness: "But goddamned people were so goddamned spoiled with the government handouts (not that you got to have none of that money, you sorry-assed bastard you) that you just couldn't get nobody that would work no goddamned more."

I got on as engineer this time. I was overjoyed about it. My old nemesis hadn't quit. He was a lifer with the company, just like the old captain, but my being on there put him on one of the other crews and I didn't have to associate with the mean son of a bitch. This little tug tried to keep three complete crews—captain, engineer, and cook-deckhand. They worked twenty days on and ten days off. On the boat, it was four hours on and four off, and, except for big deals like sinking barges and bad weather, there was only one crew on duty at the time. It was possible to completely avoid somebody on another crew if you wanted to. I turned the mattress over and settled right back in again.

Some things were different. First, though we were still on the Yankeetown run, we were towing straight out of the refinery at Chalmette, just below New Orleans. While the boat was in dry dock, the company had leased a Louisiana delta boat (commonly called "Coon Ass" boats for some bastardization of one name for French-speaking south Louisianans, which circuitous etymological trail has long been lost. If you decide to add that to your vocabulary, watch yourself, because there is another branch of French speakers in that state who call themselves "Creoles" and neither group likes to be confused with the other and nobody down there likes the English to overstep themselves). The delta boat was to take on the intracoastal work. The New Orleans boat was experienced with big, swift, crooked rivers, and they soon shooed the old *Roulette* off the Apalachicola and started taking the gas to Bainbridge and Columbus and St. Marks all in the same trip, in a route just like a potato chip truck. As soon as that happened, the old turd that owned the *Roulette* promptly went bankrupt and got a job abusing people at the state hospital in Chattahoochee. The slave hit the river swamp again.

On my first ten days off I went down there to see if I could find out what it would take to buy that old *Roulette* from the court. I found out that the boat was sunk up in a slough just off the Jackson River and would probably go pretty cheap. I borrowed a skiffboat and went to see what kind of shape the machinery was in. When I got there, I was in for a surprise.

First, only most of the hull was sunk. All the guts and the screen wire part were still sticking up above the surface (at least at that stage of the river). I wandered around looking at the junk and thinking how I could have the damn thing back to running in about two days if I could get a big pump down there, when I noticed a little pig tied by one leg to the stove. I poked around a little and found a dry box of matches and a small stash of porno magazines and I knew what was up. I left in the skiff like I was going back to Apalach, then I slipped back on the bank and caught the ex-slave feeding crawfish and fish heads to his pig.

I spent the night on there with him and we caught some stump-knockers (that's a river bream with little black specks all over him like he had already been peppered) and one speckled perch (that's "black crappie" to some) to go with his palm cabbage for supper. We got to talking about his prospects. Though the wreck of the *Roulette* was a good camp for him, it was sort of exposed to traffic in the river, and the wheelman of every tugboat that came by felt obligated to study it intensely with the carbon-arc light (a very intense light). He said that fishermen were starting to come displace him on weekends to stay in the screen wire and run trotlines and drink beer. "Wouldn't leave a full can behind for nothing," said the ex-slave. He was wondering about the prospects of getting on with us. "Y'all still got all them magazines under the seat in the galley? Reckon I'd get caught?" he wondered. "Yeah, we still got every single one and you probably would get caught but nobody would pay any attention to it. Everybody looks at those magazines," says me. "Naw, goddammit, I mean do you think somebody would find out who I was and send me back to Chattahoochee? Ain't no telling what that old asshole would do to me if I got locked up in there with him." We talked about the isolation of the tank farm in Yankeetown and how we never had much communication with any boat in the gulf, and after I told him a thing or two about New Orleans, he decided to take a chance.

He went to Chalmette and got on with one of the other crews as cook. I wanted to warn him about that mean engineer but there was hardly any opportunity. Besides, I figured, if he could deal with the captain of the *Roulette,* he wouldn't have any trouble with the second engineer of our boat. But it was a complicated situation, and the way things turned out, it would probably have been best if he had known how it was on there.

The old captain had a cataract operation that turned out not to be very satisfactory because of some disorder of the retina of both eyes. He was pretty close to his retirement time when all this happened and he knew he had to keep plugging until then. I don't know how he worked it, but he managed to keep his license even though he could barely see the bow of the barge. The mean engineer had been with him all that time. When the captain got so that he couldn't see, he and the engineer just sort of swapped jobs. When I was on the crew with them, I handled the boat in the refinery and at Yankeetown and didn't tell anybody. When I wasn't on there, the engineer knocked down the pilings at the refinery and Yankeetown and rooted up the trees along the river. I ought to give the devil his due. He was a pretty good wheelman. He wasn't the ace that I am or the old captain when he could still see, but he could, in his slow and sloppy way, get the barge to the dock. He didn't have a license and it would have been hell to pay if he had hit anything, but as the old captain had said, "What the fuck they going to do, pull my license and take my goddamn Cadillac? Hell, I'm seventy years old. I got thirty dollars, I'll catch the goddamn bus just like you with yo' sorry ass. Just go live with my daughter—at least she can cook." I said, "Look out now. Don't be complaining about the cooking. You would starve to death before you could work that first Vienna sausage out of the can as blind as you are and you never would get them saltines gummed open."

The whole criminal conspiracy would have worked fine except for one thing. The engineer was one of those damned aggressive, dangerous sodomites like you find in jails. That's how the fugitive managed to get hired so easy. There are supposed to be three men on each crew. Because of the engineer, there was usually a vacancy on that one. Mostly, that was no problem because the short towline method required a minimum of decking and both the captain and engineer were old hands at it. After the engineer ran off each new deckhand, the boat just ran shorthanded until another desperate fool like me or the fugitive showed up.

When our crew went to relieve the old captain's crew including the new cook-deckhand from his very first trip, the boat was waiting to lock out of the Mississippi into the gulf. There were a bunch of New Orleans policemen in the galley talking to the old captain and the new cook-deckhand and drinking coffee. All the business was tended to already, and the crew change out went normally except that the mean engineer was not there to be relieved. The old captain and the ex-slave got in the old raggedy company car that we had come in and drove away. The way the locking was going, it looked like I might have time to set the valves on one engine before our turn came, so I didn't get into any of the discussions but went straight down to the engine room to try to do something during that rare time when the engines weren't running. As it turned out, we had to go in the lock before I got all the valve covers back on and I had to start the engine and just let the oil run down.

By the time I got it all wiped up and washed off (never a drop in the bilge) and had a chance to come up, we were already through the lock and it was time to put the barges on the towline (barges have to be made up to push in the locks no matter what kind of hotshot short-tow man you think you are). Turned out that all the hullabaloo with the law was because the old captain's engineer had disappeared while they were tied up in Chalmette at the refinery. Couldn't find him anywhere. One theory was that he might have gone ashore and got messed up. I doubted that. The mean-assed bastard never went ashore. I always thought it was because he was afraid somebody might decide to find out just how much there was to him with all his big talk.

As it turned out, later, there wasn't quite enough. We found out that his body washed up in the bushes along the bank of one of the distributaries down in the delta. He had been cut wide open (right through the belt) with a real sharp knife. The way we found out about it was that the Coast Guard sent a helicopter to intercept us way out in the middle of the gulf. They said on the radio that they wanted "the deckhand." They let this man down on a quarter-inch cable in a bosun's chair to pick up the suspect. It was hard to communicate with him after he got down because of the racket of the helicopter and the feeling from that machine gun they had up there looking right down our noses. I was volunteered to go with him since I was the closest thing to a "deckhand" they had.

It took a long time in New Orleans, what with my crew and alibi still on the boat plugging for Yankeetown. I don't want to issue no sweeping prejudicial statement, but it's not good to get locked up in New Orleans even if you aren't the right man. I was lucky and able to stay single because of my age and the ferocity of my response to proposals, which was taken as comical by the old hands in the jail.

I finally got turned loose when my momma called up some people she knew down in the parish. Everybody apologized and went on and on about how they didn't know I was a friend of Mr. this and Miss that. By the time they finally got hot on the trail of the fugitive from Estiffanulga, he was hid out back in Tate's Hell swamp. I don't guess he would have stood a chance if they could have sent a real delta swat team up there, but those regular old Florida good-ole-boy refugees from the big-screen TV and the can of beer couldn't get far enough from the four-wheel drive and the metal flake bass boat to find him.

The embarrassment of the Coast Guard fiasco where they picked up a man from the wrong crew and the frequentness of a dead asshole floating up in the Mississippi River sort of cooled the pursuit after a while. I got transferred onto the old captain's crew and took over in the wheelhouse just about like the dead engineer. It was a good winter over all, sort of calm some trips. The old captain, without the burden of his regular engineer, hired a good man for the engine room and took over as the unofficial cook-deckhand. I couldn't help teasing him a little because his reactions were so comical, but I only got my plate taken once or twice. Actually, he was a pretty good cook, even made lasagna. About the only thing I could think of to complain about was how often we had that damned peach cobbler recipe that the slave had given us. Even though I was engineer, I had to make a few lemon meringue pies just to break the monotony. You know, a hint of diesel fuel don't hurt a pie all that much. Two men from South Carolina bought the *Roulette* from the court, put it about halfway back together, and skirted around in the shallow water next to the woods between Apalach and Tarpon Springs to take it around the peninsula through the Keys. They were trying to get to the Dismal Swamp canal where they thought they would get rich pushing in that shallow water. The whole thing was a desperate, low-budget operation. When they got to the Keys they messed up and went through, under the bridge, at channel five and into the Atlantic. I guess they were thinking that they would just ride the Gulf Stream up to the Carolinas like the big ships do and save fuel, but the waves started batting the back sides of the paddle wheels and stripped the pinion out of the differential in the truck axle and the whole mess washed up on a pretty coral reef and tore up hundreds of years of work by the tiny commensal polyps. Four or five agencies of the government tried to fine them to help pay for the salvage operation, but those fools didn't have anything to pay a fine with.

Things got to running so smooth on our old boat that it got boring. Some of the crew even went together and bought a damned TV. Fortunately we were out of range on most of the Yankeetown run, but it finally got so that the most exciting thing on there was trying to find the place to drive another stob in the bottom. When I finally got tired of standing up there in the wheelhouse listening to all those people with cartoon-character voices on the radio and decided to jump ship again, the old, blind, toothless captain still had about seven or eight months to go to get his pension. I was itching to go (had complete, full-size patterns for a set of molds for a sailboat under my mattress), but I couldn't leave the old man in such a fix as that. What he needed was a good reliable wheelman who didn't communicate with the authorities too much. Soon as crew change came, I went to Apalach and borrowed the same skiffboat as the other time and headed up the river.

It was spring by then and the mighty Apalachicola was high and swift from all the rain. It took me a long time to get up beyond the mouth of the Jackson River, because I had to stop to dump the water out of that silly-assed, aluminum, butt-head skiff (called, appropriately, a "Honkey Drownder" by black folks around here) a bunch of times. It had metal-fatigued and split all along the bottom of the transom and the duct tape was coming loose. Once I had to take the spark plugs out of the nine-point-nine when I waited too long and the boat sank and immersed the engine. It was dark and cold when I finally came to the place where we used to tie up the *Roulette*'s empty barge. It didn't take me long to smell smoke and slip up on my man so I could back up to his fire while we cut us a deal.

The last time I saw him was in New Orleans. He was driving the captain's old Cadillac convertible down the street, just as bold as brass. He had two very fat, freckle-faced, redheaded ladies in the backseat holding up those little celluloid whirligig propellers like we used to give children at parties a long time ago. I couldn't tell if they were coming from a party or if it was just getting started.

Here is the slave's recipe:

Peach Cobbler

While you preheat the oven, put the frying pan on top of the stove and melt one whole stick of butter in it (I said butter, not yellow-colored Crisco . . . which during WWII they packaged the coloring stuff separately . . . ain't got it the right color yet). While the butter is melting, open two cans of peaches and drink the juice out of one can. Pour the rest—peaches and syrup—in with the butter and turn off the fire. Broadcast a whole handful of flour, more or less evenly, on top of the butter and peaches, then sprinkle a whole handful of sugar on top of that. Poke it around a little bit but don't stir. Put the frying pan in the oven and look at the porno magazines until the sugar gets good and brown. It'll make you fat if you don't look out . . . but it won't make you redheaded and freckled all over.

ISLANDS

in which I reveal yet another obsession

I LOVE ISLANDS AND have ever since I was a little boy. I think it is a natural human instinct that, if not stultified by the maturation process, is apt to persist right on up into old age. I used to build islands when I was a child. Down at our old coasthouse there was this little dark water marsh creek that ran across the beach every time it had been raining much. I used to ditch and dam until I forced it to divide into two distributaries as it crossed the wide, white sand . . . made an island for myself. Pretty soon, my expeditions of exploration on my property would have it completely covered with my tracks. Man can't do much better than that to mark what he owns.

You can occupy ready-made islands, too. When my boys were little, because of my persistence in the boatbuilding business, we were real poor and couldn't afford to go to resorts and theme parks and stuff like that, so we went on long expeditions to islands either in the new *Nueva Eva* or in a car with a little boat on top. First we would go to the surveyor's office and pore over the quadrangles to find islands that were not on regular maps, then we would load up our camping junk and head out. I ain't going to tell you where all of those islands are so when my grandchildren start looking for them, they won't find all of y'all covering them up like wasps on the nest in the late summer. But I will tell you about one good place.

Right off the defunct (thank goodness) Cross Florida Barge Canal south of Yankeetown and north of Crystal River are some of the most charming little islands in the world. Some of them aren't much bigger than a car but are high and dry and rocky with pretty deep water (ain't much water anywhere down there) right up to the bank so you can tie up like to a dock. The first time we went there was in the summer and we had forgotten our shoes. We wanted to walk all over and around every one of those zillion little islands, but they were rocky and sharp (a lot like the Bahamas). Finally, we sat down and wove us some shoes out of palmetto fronds—good shoes, too—nothing better for wading as the water and sand can just run out the bottom. When a hole gets worn in the heel or the ball of the foot, it's just the work of a minute to recap that place. We ate good, too. There was a stone crab under every rock. There were plenty of oysters, clams, and blue crabs, and the fishing was very good right off the bank. There were some running peas growing on the beach; looked just about like regular field peas with pale blue flowers. We could have stayed down there forever if it hadn't been for school and boatbuilding . . . insurance payments, electric bills, taxes, and Santa Claus.

The only thing wrong with that place was that every night, a whole scad of very impertinent coons would swim over from the mainland and rampage all over every single one of those islands. As the sun went down, you could see them coming . . . hundreds of little intense faces heading our way . . . kind of intimidating to those who know coons. They were so brave that I believe that if you didn't keep the tent door zipped up, they would pull you out of the bed and feel you all over with their little busy hands looking for something edible. At any rate, we could hardly sleep for all of them chewing and squabbling out there—had to catch a little catch-up snooze after the sun came up and they swam back—ears sticking up in profile against the glare of the rising sun.

When I was towing fuel oil and gasoline into the little tank farm in Yankeetown or the big power plant at Crystal River . . . had to pass right by our little place and I would get homesick. Sometimes I could even see the coons early in the morning or late in the afternoon and one night, I swung the old carbon arc search-light around and illuminated one of the little islands and the sight of all those little bright-eyed faces just about snatched a knot in my heart. . . . Dang.

The island I live on now ain't much more than that, actually much less stable . . . just a sandbar out in the Gulf of Mexico about three and a half miles from the mainland. Every time we have much of a storm, the sea washes clear across and shifts the island's position relative to our house . . . kind of keeps a man from getting too big for his britches. Lots of the other houses over here (some regular big deal outfits, too) have had the island move right on out of the yard and leave them standing temporarily in the breakers of the open ocean . . . temporarily not because the island came back again, but because the sea does not go easy on such a thing as a house, no matter what kind of big deal outfit it was. For some reason our little shanty, which we knew was temporary when we throwed it up, still has some sand piled up around it (knock wood). As a matter of fact, some of those other people's land has washed down here with us and our once tiny lot is now pretty big. . . . Won't gloat, though, because it might be gone tomorrow, or the county will find out about it and raise the taxes.

One time, a house over here wound up in the water and it was a temporary situation of the other kind. Before the whole house was bashed into smithereens and strewed all up and down the beach, some kind of eddy or other put the sand right back where it was—but not before the surf tore off the big deal elaborate steps. It was sort of mystifying to the owner, who spent the whole time all this was going on in federal prison for some impropriety involving large sums of money and some drugs. When he came back, there was his house, seemingly just as before except that the fancy steps were completely gone. He couldn't get into his house. I am afraid I watched him through the binoculars as he tried to climb one piling after the other as if the next one was going to be easier. Finally he trudged off down the sand bed that these fools over here call a road and borrowed (stole) a ladder from another house. Normally this would be the end of the story, but it gets worse. I heard (I don't communicate with little jerks like that unless I want to carry it to fruition) that he was skulking around over on the mainland somewhere and found his steps on another house. They must have drifted ashore after the storm and someone decided to claim them as flotsam. The little criminal thought the man had come to the island and stolen those steps off of his house. Anyway, this little fool got hopping mad and made some threats or something to the man with the steps. The funny thing was that the man he was threatening was the prosecutor of the county and got the little criminal's parole revoked and sent his ass to Walla Walla, Washington. The house still ain't got no steps and somebody restole the ladder. No telling what will happen next. There will be plenty of time, though. I heard twenty years.

One batch of our grandchildren is big enough to take care of themselves at the coast now, and like we used to be, they are long gone right after breakfast and not likely to come back until no telling when. We just had the spring tides of the full moon. The main low was about 9:00 P.M. The children did not show up when it got dark. My wife and I set off across the wide flats following the yellow brick road to the moon. We thought we saw some coons marauding in their intent, busy way out on the wet sand down by the mouth of the big marsh creek. When we got closer, we recognized the three children acting just exactly like coons. They were on all fours, butts sticking way up, and digging furiously. They didn't even see us as we walked close enough to see what they were doing. The light of the full moon revealed that they were busily maintaining moat creeks of sparkling water around each of their three islands. We were able to slip away without being seen. Ain't no telling when they came in, but I bet it was after the tide rose and took their property away from them.

THE CANNED HAM INCIDENT

in which I do not participate, so Hurrah for the other side

I GUESS IT WAS about 1985 when I heard this story from a permanent resident of this island. Given that I was not an eyewitness, some of the accuracy may be in doubt, but it ain't the kind of thing that is normally embellished too much and the details are all too bizarre to invent—all highly technical stuff, so if you ain't into that, better skip on. This is a long, long story . . . takes about three hours, what with kibitzing, to tell it right, but I'll try to cut it to the very bone.

There was a preacher from Missouri, or someplace like that, who got some supporters to outfit a missionary project, and he built a big pirate-ship-looking thing to sail down the Mississippi to the Caribbean to save the heathens down there. He had already made it down the Mississippi and east as far as he could go and still stay out of the open ocean. Though I was not a participant in the actual incident in question, I did see the ship docked in Carrabelle at the eastern terminus of the North Gulf Intracoastal Waterway, where he was fueling up to head outside for the first time across the gulf of the northeastern bend of Florida. You know, just that he had come all that way says something for the man and his ship. Errol Flynn would have been right at home on that thing. It looked like the boat was almost fifty feet long, but it was hard to tell where the actual boat stopped and the decorative part started. It had all sorts of filigree and dolphin strikers and chicken beaks and stuff up by the head and some sort of balcony and extra transom and windows back by the stern enclosing the enormous head of what would normally have been an outboard rudder. The kitchen was way up in the forecastle . . . on deck with full standing room and a regular-size cast iron, combination L.P. and wood-burning range. The living quarters were in the poop and had the rudderhead protruding up through the roof with a twenty-some-odd-foot tiller way up there seven or eight feet off the deck. It was worked by hauling tackles to a homemade spoked wheel, at least seven feet tall, mounted on a preaching pulpit in front of the forward bay windows of the living quarters. The well-lit cabin must have been a delightful place with all those windows and all those Bibles and hymnals and prayer books in shelves lining the walls, their spines gleaming with gold. There were two huge masts that looked just like pressure-treated utility poles with varnish on them. I noticed an ingenious use of semi-truck mudflaps as chafing gear for the gigantic yards lashed to the masts and secured at the ends by braces and the sheets that would normally be made up to the clew corners of the sails. The preacher was even kind enough to take me below to show me the stores and the engine room. I noticed hundreds of canned hams stored under a grating in the dry and spotless bilge, and boxes of spaghetti in racks along the sides of the hull. Big agricultural liquid tanks gleamed palely up in the bow. There were cardboard boxes of even more Bibles, hymnals, and prayer books secured with big rope netting. The immaculate engine room had a little Perkins diesel engine . . . heat exchanger cooled, three-to-one "Velvet Drive" gear, 1⅜-inch stainless shaft, patent, "never-drip" hard-seal well-pump-style stuffing box. There were at least two fuel filters and a sediment bowl. A big old polished bronze and glass raw water strainer glistened like jewelry in the fluorescent lights. I was able to catch a glimpse of the dull but expensive gleam of no-telling-how-many genuine Rolls batteries under the stainless steel expanded metal of the engine room deck. There was a paper towel holder handy to the dipstick. Bounty paper towels—there was nothing second rate down there. Errol might have fit in pretty good on deck, but you could tell, that preacher wouldn't have let him penetrate ever so slightly into that engine room with his slap-dash self. I even felt a little out of place, but I was glad to get a chance to marvel at it.

I liked his engine room and agreed with him about his mission. Somebody needed to do something about all those heathens down in the Caribbean islands. I told that preacher that I thought the way to do it would be to clench a Bible, hymnal, or prayer book in his teeth and swing over onto the heathen yacht on a halyard with a canned ham under his arm. I hope I don't give the impression that I am making fun of the man. His boat might have been something of a show and I guess that is what he thought it would take to accomplish his mission. It was obvious that he knew exactly what he was doing, so far, and I'm sure he knew exactly how to deal with heathens without me. Unfortunately, I had to come back to our shop in Georgia to try to build a boat for a man and was unable to supervise the crossing of the open water of the northeastern Gulf of Mexico . . . too bad.

The way I heard it from my islander buddy, the preacher listened to the droning, on and on, of the National Weather Service and looked at the weather fax until it looked like it would be good for a while and then motored out the pass between St. George and Dog islands into the open gulf, heading for where the intracoastal waterway resumed at Anclote Key about a hundred miles away. He was planning to motor the whole way like he had been doing so far and save his sails for "the trades." He listened to the radio too long, though, and missed the tide in the pass, and by the time that little 4-108 had pushed that behemoth out past all that water coming in, it was getting late. Later he told my buddy, one of Dog Island's hard-bitten permanent residents, that he was counting on the land breeze to give him a nice lee of the island and the shoals east of there to make it an easy cruise. It probably would have been a nice trip in a more predictable season of the year. After the preacher got outside the pass in the nice easy swells of the big water, he activated the autopilot and went into his house and got a chair and his bedroom slippers and sat there watching his great big wheel turning ever so slightly in tune to the flux gate and watched the Floridians turn on all those electric lights that they use to demonstrate their dominion over nature. I guess he was thinking about opening up one of them canned hams when the wind started breezing up from the south a little like it does around here when a cold front whips a little farther down than expected and begins to draw the weather in from the gulf. By the time he got the chair and the bedroom slippers secured, it was blowing pretty good. Too bad it wasn't the expected land-breeze and there wasn't any lee. The preacher said that it was blowing about fifty with fifteen- to twenty-foot swells. The data buoy anchored eighty miles out in the gulf said eighteen with gusts to twenty-two and four- to six-foot waves, but you know, things are real variable in the Gulf of Mexico.

About midnight or so, my buddy, the permanent resident of the island, was coming home across the bay. I guess I better explain that situation. This island where I live most of the time has no bridge or public transportation to it. Because of that and certain other characteristics (like intermittent electricity), there are only a few people who live here all the time. Most of the folks over here just come on weekends when the weather is good and the FSU "Noles" ain't playing. It takes a special person to be able to handle this place. So, this friend of mine was coming back to the island in his motor whaleboat from checking in at the Tiki Bar (a little bar right on the river with roaches in the palm-thatched cabanas—to enhance the ambiance) on the mainland, which he sometimes visited for a little while, when he noticed eleven very bright flares from somewhere around the shoals east of the island. He knew that a vessel was in distress—big-time, from the quantity and quality of those flares—so he headed to the rescue and found the preacher and his boat washed up sideways on the sandbar (called "Dog Island Reef" on the charts). Turned out that, while he was skirting the windward side of the shoals watching his GPS and Loran and radar wondering when the land breeze would start up, the beam sea began rolling those telephone poles around in the holes until they wallowed the wedges out and then they really went to flopping. Before long, the yards had snatched enough slack in the lines securing them so that they were trying to sweep all that tophamper off the deck. There was nothing the preacher could do but hold on to the wheel and try to give the autopilot and that little Perkins all the help he could while he dodged those spars. He would have probably managed to slide by the shoals if one of the canned hams hadn't hopped over and popped the nipple off the "state-of-the art" plastic (I ain't gonna mention no names but I am a bronze-age man myself) raw water intake through-the-hull fitting to the engine. After that, it didn't take long to boil all the coolant out of the heat exchanger. The preacher was too busy to notice until the engine ran hot and seized and the whole mess washed sideways up on the bar. The preacher dove for his emergency cabinet and all those (not out-of-date) SOLAS-approved flares. Would have shot an even dozen but he dropped one while he was side-skipping the sweep of the main yard. My buddy says he was amazed at the spectacle of just eleven of those things. Said, "You know them little shotgun-shell flares like go in the plastic pistol, just ain't in it with the real thing."

When my buddy got there, the big boat was lying over on its side with its bottom to the breakers in about four or five feet of water. My buddy eased the whaleboat around to the lee side and tried to hold a conversation with the preacher about what he wanted to do. Turned out that he should have just told him to hop on board if he wanted to go back to Carrabelle because the man refused to abandon all those Bibles. While they were trying to shift the good books from one boat to the other in the surf, that one-inch fitting in the bottom of the big boat was equalizing

the inside water level with the outside water level (both well above
the batteries), which killed all three radios (single-sideband, VHF,
and CB) and left only the meaningless drone of the dry-cell-
powered weather radio. The wind shift from the cold front came,
the tide turned and took the wreck off the reef, where it sank down
to where the spars and part of the preacher were all that were
sticking out.

It took a while for the preacher to convince himself that it was
all right now to give up the good fight and get out of that cold
water. Unbeknownst to both of them, during the decision making
process, the whaleboat was winding up six hundred feet of half-
inch nylon line with its propeller. My buddy finally figured it out
when a big inflatable boat appeared, coming rapidly up from
astern. The cold, the Tiki Bar, and the frustration of trying to be
subtle with this preacher had dimmed his wits, and at first he
thought this thing was just coming to see how things were going
when, in fact, it wanted to dive under the stern of the whaleboat,
explode, and wrap all up in the wheel in a knot as hard as a truck
tire. He and the preacher spent a long time trying to cut the damn
thing loose, but they were frustrated by the coldness of the water,
the toughness of the fabric of the top-notch dinghy, and by a five-
horse British Seagull outboard motor that was also wrapped
around the wheel and shaft of the whaleboat. By the time they
gave up on trying to clear the propeller, the Seagull was all they
could get loose. Too bad the "stopped lark's head" the preacher
had tied around the mast of the ship to make up the whaleboat
didn't hold like that knot around the propeller, and they had been
drifting rapidly toward the Florida Middle Ground all this time.
They tried the old trusty 12H Danforth which had held the whale-

boat so faithfully for so many years in the rough anchorage at Dog Island, but it wouldn't find the bottom with the line that they had close to hand. Of course, they had the six-hundred-foot dinghy painter spooled up between the wheel and the strut, but that was unavailable. My buddy estimated that they would end up somewhere down around Ft. Myers if they were really lucky. If they were just sort of lucky and the wind came on around more east like it usually did, it would be the Keys or Cuba. If they weren't lucky, they might get to work with the heathens after all. Hard to predict on the first day of a four- or five-day norther.

My buddy finally brought all his faculties to bear on the problem and decided to try to get the Seagull running. The muffler was gone, the shaft was bent in a U, two of the five propeller blades were busted off (all on the same side, wouldn't you know), and the whole steering handle–throttle control arrangement was gone. Not only that, but it looked like something had been snatched out of the carburetor by the throttle cable. Only after they had taken the foot off and straightened the little square tubing thing that the Seagull factory uses for a shaft between the head and the foot, and beat the housing back into some kind of shape that would allow a little strained rotation, did they discover that the crankshaft was bent so that the flywheel was jammed against the magneto stator plate. (Y'all following all this? Might better read back over it or the rest ain't going to make a bit of sense.) They finally straightened it out so that it could wobble almost clear by driving screwdrivers up under the rim of the flywheel and prying against the stator plate and the face of the core of the coil.

My buddy had five gallons of gas that he was carrying to the island for his generator, but there wasn't any oil. He was very proud of the integrity of the whaleboat's own 4-108 and felt that the display of gallon jugs of Delo 400 was undignified in a good boat. They had to break the antenna off the weather radio to use as a straw to suck the black oil out of the dipstick hole of the whaleboat's engine with their lips. My buddy, an old mariner for real, said that that sucking business was the closest he ever came to being seasick in his life, but he had to do it. Luckily, the preacher was up to the job, too, so they took turns sucking on the antenna. They mixed the oil with the gas a little at a time in a cut-off bleach-jug bailer and poured it in the Seagull's squashed gas tank. Then they tried to crank it while it was clamped onto one of the interior bulkheads of the whaleboat . . . no spark . . . so they turned it upside down and poured gas all up under the flywheel to try to flush out some of the water from the points and coil and all. When they pulled the rope after that, the old Seagull fired right off . . . literally. . . . Those SOLAS flares were puny compared to the fireball that came out from under the flywheel of that Seagull.

So there it was running, wide open (the thing that had been jerked out of the carburetor by the throttle cable turned out to have been the throttle itself) in a pool of flaming gasoline. My buddy said it was hard not to back up to the fire for a little while in that cold wind in his wet clothes. Finally, the out-of-balance of the wobbling flywheel, the bent shaft, the broke propeller, and the nature of the Seagull itself combined to vibrate the clamps loose and the whole bellowing mess fell off the bulkhead into the fire, where the oxygen finally burned up enough to shut it down. Of course, the impact knocked some of the paper towel (not Bounty) stuffing out of the holes in the gas tank and added more gas to the fire, which increased the draft so that my buddy and the preacher had to dance around quite a bit to avoid the flames that were whipped every which-a-way by the increasing north wind. Unfortunately, they had chosen the bulkhead that the fire extinguisher was mounted on for their mechanicking. Luckily those old surplus whaleboats are made out of fire retardant resin or their gooses would have been cooked. Finally, all the wasted gas burned up and they were able to proceed to step two—after they had sucked some more oil out of the dipstick hole with their lips.

I'm going to try to cut this thing down as best I can, but there is only so much that can be left out. . . . What finally happened is that they nailed the cut-bait board to the stern of the double-ended, thick fiberglass whaleboat so that it wobbled sort of catty-wampus off to one side and clamped the Seagull to it and tied it off to the towing bit to help the nails hold a little longer between re-nailing and motored off into the cold wind. It was a slow trip, but they didn't get bored. They found that they had a steady job sucking oil out of the crankcase of the whaleboat's engine. They were mixing gas by instinct and scared to death that they might starve the Seagull of oil and gall the liner and rings, and maybe even seize the already overstressed crankshaft, and then, considering the way the wind had veered, it would be the heathens of Africa for sure, so they sucked hard. The colder it got, the thicker the oil became. When they cranked the Diesel to warm the oil up a little so it would be easier to suck, the dipstick hole pooted little droplets of black oil right in their faces, but that was an insignificant thing in the face of the rest of all this. Finally, in the desperate scramble to transport the open container of precious mix and pour it into the out-of-reach gas tank of the crazily wiggling Seagull, one of them bumped into the whaleboat's gearshift, and instead of instantly choking the engine down against the fouled propeller, the old whaleboat began to motor ahead. It turns out that all the pitching and rolling from the rough seas had unwiggled the Avon from the wheel, unwound the six hundred feet of line, and they were under way, upwind in a forty-horsepower motor whaleboat built just exactly for that kind of duty. They hooked all forty of them horses up, pried the baitboard off the stern, let all that foolishness go to the bottom, and headed for Dog Island. They got there just in time for the arrival of the 11:00 A.M. private ferry. "Man, what happened to Y'all's faces?" said the wit that met them trudging up the dock.

Epilogue

(I'll cut this to the bone, too.) They went back and re-floated the "Heathen's Revenge" with two waterbeds inflated in the hold by a scuba tank and sold it and divided up the revenue in an agreeable fashion. The preacher went back to Missouri and my buddy went back to the Tiki Bar.

DEAD MAN'S BOAT

in which I reveal two morals

I HAVE NEVER BEEN more reverent for people after they are dead than I was when they were alive. I mean, it just don't make any sense to me to overlook the facts of the matter. Might as well not hold back on a good story just because the person it is about ain't around to enjoy it.

About 1989 I built a boat for an old, old friend of mine and he was just about on his last legs when he ordered this boat. He already had three of my boats, and though he was so decrepit that he wasn't able to use any of them when he ordered this one, he didn't think he was quite through yet. What he wanted this time was a tiny pirogue. He said that he was going to get his grand-daughters to take him down to his pond and lay him out in the bottom of it (he specified that it have no thwarts), cover him with his wool afghan, and push him out away from the bank to drift in the sun every now and then when the weather was fine for what he was sure was his last winter in Georgia. I dropped everything and went to work, but in spite of that, I was too late.

I had invented this way to make these little extra-light model-bow pirogues a long time ago and they were hot sellers among high-card duck hunters who owned swampland down in south Louisiana. The way they were built was that the whole bottom of the boat was made out of two wide poplar (tulip poplar, *Liriodendron tulipifera*) boards that were carved so that they were kind of thick along the edges in the wide part of the boat to form sort of a chine to fasten the sides to but were tapered thin at the ends so that they could be pulled up to the stems to form a hollow entry and fine place at the stern to ease loose of the water. The bottom board of the sides fastened along the bottom planking chine-style in the middle and then rolled around so that the forward and aft of the boat became lap-strake with rebates where the planks joined the stem and sternpost. Though there were only two topside planks to the side, the flexibility of the poplar allowed me to get a good flare and made a pretty good-looking little pirogue (if I do say so myself). I built them in two versions—"standard" and "extra-light." A twelve-foot standard one, some three feet wide only weighed thirty pounds or so and the lightest one that same size only weighed nineteen—but then the sides weren't but about nine inches high in the middle. You can say that such a thing is too little to be useful if you want to, but down where the pirogue is (or used to be) the true tool, it ain't uncommon for two big men to stand up in one littler than that and each shoot a twelve-gauge shotgun out the same side (at baited ducks on the water before legal daylight, most likely). Of course, the water is so shallow most places that if they had to step out for a minute to catch their balance, they would hardly get their cowboy boots wet.

So my old friend had always wanted to figure out why he needed one of those little boats and it is too bad that he was dead before he finally got his chance. When I heard that he had what was certainly his final stroke, I went to the family and told them that they needed to feel no obligation to me for the almost finished little boat, but they assured me that there was nothing that the old man would want better than for them to take it. They said that when he finished dying, they would dress up the littlest of the great-granddaughters and let her take his ashes out into the pond in it and let him fly. I went out on the side porch where they had him lying in a hospital bed to see if I couldn't get one last rise out of him, but even my little statuette of the Venus of Willendorf failed to move him and I knew I needed to hurry back to the shop and get to work.

Everything would have turned out all right except for his youngest son. He has three sons whom I knew well because they were in my cabin at the Y camp three summers in a row. All three of them were wild for adventures in the woods, creeks, and swamps around the camp, and my cabin of boys always came back more muddy and scratched up than all the others and were sometimes late for supper. Two of those boys have slowed down enough to function fine in the regular world, but the youngest turned out to be one of those people who is just too enthusiastic to adapt well. He has been wrapped up to the eyeballs in more wild schemes and reckless jobs than anybody I know, most of them somehow involving paint.

One time he had a job painting the inside of the pipes leading water to the turbines under Boulder Dam in Colorado. He told me all about it. He had to crawl about a mile through this eighteen-inch pipe dragging his paint, a big electric hot plate, a long extension cord, and an air hose. Once he got to the place where he left off last time, he cooked his paint on the hot plate until it was blistering hot and lay on his back while he daubed all around the inside of the pipe. As he worked, he had to rearrange his air hose to blow enough air on him so that he could continue to live and he had to backtrack to drag the hose and extension cord out of his way. He said that the whole business was a pain in the ass but that he made enough money in some four or five months to buy a good used Corvette and make a trip way down into Mexico almost to Nicaragua, where it was stolen along with all his belongings—he had to hitchhike back to Panacea. But, like the old song, "It was worth it for the time that I had," he said. After that job, he painted television and water towers and even had a job spraying logos on blimps. He was a regular paint man, and when his father died, he was in the newly discovered poly-urethane varnish business (now he buys surplus Navy paint and sells it to boatyards all up and down the East Coast out of his sailboat).

His family always had plenty of confidence in him and sup-ported every one of his adventurous notions, so they insisted that I varnish the little pirogue with his product. I had been epoxyfying my boats for quite a while by then but was still using automotive clear-coat acrylic lacquer to protect the epoxy from the sun (which works pretty good). The son had told me of the wonders of this polyurethane, and though talk is cheap, I was anxious to try it out, and since these people were perfectly willing to take the burden of proof on themselves, I sprayed the little boat. It wet out and flowed into itself so well that I was astonished. The spray gun worked better, too. The recommended viscosity would have made a mess of a lacquer job, but though it stayed liquid so long that it absorbed the overspray most miraculously, there were no curtains, runs, or orange peel. If it could stand the weather like it was supposed to, it would certainly be the trick for protecting solventless epoxy.

After the solvent flashed out, I laid on another coat. There was no sign of any tendency to curtain, so I turned up the heat and let her rip again. After the solvent of the third coat had evaporated, I measured a miraculously uniform wet-film thickness of between five or six mils all over the whole boat and, considering the circumstances, decided to stop right there. Wow, it shined like a diamond in a goat's ass.

The next morning it was still gleaming in there. We had just had a good rain to cut down the pollen (chased the old man's barbecuing wake inside) and my dust machine had worked good. Except for one or two bug turds, I had a perfect varnish job. The coating was still soft enough for me to pick out the turds and swipe the place with my wet finger. I called the family and told them that I probably wouldn't be able to deliver the boat until the next morning and they said that that would be fine because they were having such a good time remembering the old man that they were in no hurry. "Might as well come eat some of these Apalachicola oysters with us while you are waiting." I went, too, and stayed mighty late because I met another old man who had served on board of a patrol boat as engineer for the old man during WWI and we got to talking. He was an amateur machinist and was just about to finish up a little Stuart Turner 5A steam engine that he had been working on for over a year. I told him that I had just the boat for it waiting for the varnish to get dry.

I can see that this story is fixing to get out of hand, so I'll cut it short. Next morning, the damned pirogue was still sticky and the wake was about ready to disperse, so I gingerly took it to the pond and spread out a piece of plastic on the bottom for the little girl (about four years old) in her pinafore. She set the urn in front of her on the sticky bottom of the boat and took up the double paddle. Though she had only had a little pirogue experience, it had sprung up a good breeze of fair wind and she set off for the middle of the pond to the cheers of all the old man's relatives and friends. We could see her busily strewing ashes on all sides. The whole operation looked a little like dervish work but she got it done. We all ran around to the lee side of the pond for her triumphant arrival. From the looks of the boat and her, I don't think but about half of the old man made it to the water. It took me five gallons of acetone to get him and that varnish off the boat.

There are two morals to this story: one is never to trust the compatibility of two wonder substances until you do the experiments, and the other is don't wait until you are dead to do your messing.

THE OLD J 80 JOHNSON

in which I help a man recover his long-lost self-esteem

THE MAIN GOAL in my life is to get to the day when I can quit burning gasoline. When I was a young man, I loved anything that burned the stuff and chased those machines with the same fervor that some young men chase women. I guess the same physiology drives both desires because . . . well . . . Anyhow, it ain't the same anymore but I still get a slight twitch when I see a little outboard motor.

An old man came to the shop with an old boogered-up outboard right about the time I shipped my last boat in August of '99. I normally stop trying to con people into letting me build them one of these boats around that time of year so I can have time to do my logging and sawmill work—and go to the coast in that wonderfully cool and biologically significant time of year, so I agreed to fix the old motor for this man just for a little spare change. He had an interesting story: It seems that when he was a young man, he had borrowed this engine from his grandfather. Because he was young and had other things on his mind, he neglected to return it until it had froze and busted. It was one of those old outboards that have a brass piston water pump driven off of a cam on the propeller shaft. Since it is a positive displacement rig, the water squirts out of the pee-hole in a regular, strong cyclic way at the rate of about three strokes of the piston to the squirt (is this a metaphor?) and all the water does not drain back out of the engine when you shut it off unless you take out a little tap down on the foot that says "Drain." If you don't do that, when it freezes, it makes a hell of a mess.

It was an old Johnson from back in the days when "horsepower" was just beginning to be used to misdescribe the capability of a machine. This old thing was bragged up to be about one hp in the days when people knew what a horse could do. No doubt, there were some who, after trying one out, raised their eyebrows when it could hardly push the boat through a patch of weeds that a one horsepower horse could have hauled out of the pond and spread on the field for manure. Now I have a "5 peak hp" vacuum cleaner that runs on twenty-two-gauge wire. It might blow hot air as hard as a horse but not like five—not when they are at their peak anyway. That ain't got nothing to do with this story, though.

What had happened was that my customer had ruined his granddaddy's old Johnson and all his life had felt guilty about it. Though he didn't say it, I bet his grandfather had never let him forget. Now, this man, a successful businessman, retired, had gotten tired of looking at the old motor that he kept as some sort of override limit on his happiness. Somehow he had found out about the twitch I get at the sight of such and had brought the damned thing to me. "Can you fix it back to where it is as good as it was before it froze and busted?" he said.

"Does a sanctified Baptist love a shiny new SUV?" said me. When I got it all taken apart ("Carb Cleaner" in the aerosol can, $1.69 for two at AutoZone is just the ticket) I found out that what was busted was the pump housing in the foot, the watertight clamp thing that held the foot on to the brass pipe that went up to the head, the tubes that conveyed the water up every whichaway to the cylinder—and the damned base of the crankcase where the water went into the engine of the thing. I fixed the water pump by turning a little liner sleeve to fit the undamaged piston. I replaced the busted tubes. I welded the aluminum foot clamp after about five tries (old 1920s aluminum is strange stuff), cut new threads, and reworked the seal, but I was stymied about the busted crankcase bottom until I remembered a brilliant genius with whom I used to work back in the tugboat days. He cast a brand-new one for me. Ain't life sweet?

The old motor ran good, too—first pull, hot or cold—though you had to work the choke and single needle valve with some expertise. My grandchildren and I took it to Lake Iamonia on my old Grumman Sport boat to see what it was like. Though it thrummed the aluminum pretty good, it didn't vibrate nearly as bad as I expected. It is one of those primitive old slow-speed, two-cycle engines that aspirates right into the cast-iron cylinder when the little two-inch piston opens the port at the bottom of the stroke. Since the fuel doesn't go through the crankcase like modern two-cycle engines, all that is lubricated by an expostulation of oil and gasoline (eight ounces, a small Coca-Cola bottle, to the gallon) from the cylinder at each compression stroke through little tubes all through the engine—kind of marvelous. There are no seals on anything (except a regular adjustable, leather packing gland, "Chicago Rawhide" on the propeller shaft) and that makes it smoke out from under the flywheel a little bit while it is cold—but when it warms up, it is cleaner running than a British Seagull. It has a dry exhaust and you can see how much it is smoking and lean it on down with the big-knob-style needle valve. Got a big aluminum take-apart muffler sort of like a Model T, which it is good to avoid when you have to tilt it, that and the spark plug and the flywheel. It is a lot like handling a crab.

I had it running in my garbage can rig when the man came back. He watched it for a while, then he gave me a check and said, "You keep that thing."

THE SAILING, COMMERCIAL FISHING FELUCCA "BULLET" # 9999

in which there is a poem

I HAVE BEEN BUILDING a little sailboat for over a year now, which is unusual for me since I am able to throw them out like McDonald's does French fries . . . well, three or four a year anyway. The reason this one took so long is that it was intended as a nonprofit job (unlike all the others, which are intended as get-rich-quick jobs), and had to be set aside while paying work was going on. After I finished the hull, it had to hang in the ceiling of the shop as out-of-the-way as I could get it. It turned out not to be quite out-of-the-way enough. I have a bunch of creases in my skull where I clipped the bronze cutwater or the sternpost guard (it is a double-ender) while I was staggering around trying to work. I actually launched the boat on 9/9/99 just for the hell of it, but have just now (Thanksgiving weekend) had time to rig and sail the little thing.

It is twelve feet long by fifty-four inches wide, another one of the little sailing double-enders that I love so much. It is a funny thing how people react to a double-ended boat. Some say, "Oh, what a nice little strip-planked canoe" (even though the boat is lap-strake). "That thing sho' is build flimsy for a pirogue," remark others. I have even heard, "I see you have a peapod theah," from one or two. Some of them get downright pedantic about it and want to say "stem and post." Well, it ain't none of those . . . it is sort of a felucca, like in the photograph by J. P. Shaw in Chappelle's *American Small Sailing Craft.* . . . It is mine and I can call it whatever I, dammit, please. I am already very fond of it and the thing I like best is that it can't burn any gas. I hate to burn gasoline. You know how some people become crazily obsessed when they get old. I think that might be my thing. "If the Almighty had meant for us to burn gas," I'll say, "he would have put a Piezo sparker on our tailbone."

The boat is built by our standard method: quarter-sawn tulip poplar planking (only ⅛-inch thick on this one) with all the planks pre-formed and heat-sheathed on both sides with epoxy and fiberglass so that the sheathing extends between the laps, making a six-ply wood-glass laminated stringer at every plank edge, so it's a light, strong boat. Though the hull weight of this one is only thirty pounds, a big, fat man (I ain't going to mention any names) can stumble all around on the thin planking even without the full, tight-fitting floorboards. The construction method is about the only thing "standard" about this boat, though.

For one thing, it is built as a commercial fishing boat. When I was in college, I worked my major field in the vague direction of "fisheries biology" so that I could use my scrambled genius to help feed the multitudes from the vast resources of the sea. Just about the time I was getting ready to top it the knob on the higher and deeper part, I realized that advancements in fishing technology were already doing too good a job eliminating what little was left from all those centuries of overfishing by primitive means and that the fishermen sure didn't need any help from me. I switched to oceanography to try to help the other side. Before long, I realized that the best way to do that would be to leave the poor critters alone. I have never gotten over the commercial fishing itch, though. I think that, like hunting and subsistence farming, fishing for a living is a natural thing for people to do and all this abstract fooling around we do now just ain't satisfactory. That's why people act so silly. If there is no point to what you do, you might as well become a consumer.

Because my peculiar notions won't let me hook up a bottom trawl behind my old Navy motor whaleboat and pull all night long to catch ten pounds of shrimp and kill hundreds of pounds of "trash," I decided that a throw (cast) net was the only acceptable way to fish commercially. At least, you can turn loose anything you don't want without hurting it real bad. My mother taught me how to throw when I was a child and my fascination with the thing has stayed with me all my life. She used to raise free-range chickens. They could fly like quail and roosted way up in the tops of tall pine trees. It might seem to some that it would be impossible to harvest such livestock until you saw her step out from behind a baited bush with her throw net. I don't want to brag, but I have become so good that all the fish in the sea are just my free-range chickens waiting for me to come throw that net over them. I have thought about going commercial for a long time. Certain feasibility studies have proven that it is a viable option for me, too. This felucca is the end result of a lifetime of research.

What I figured to do was to catch enough fish to pay for the gas to maintain my forked lifestyle—the one where I build boats up here in Georgia half the time and research boat performance down at the coast the other half. My old junkpile car burns about thirteen bucks each round-trip. That's only six or seven two-dollar fish—easy money for an ace like me. The only thing wrong is that I have now decided that I don't think it is right to sell any kind of wild thing. I wouldn't want to impose my notions on anybody else, but I feel that if you want to eat a wild fish, you ought to get off your dead ass and go catch you one and you ought not to catch any more than you need, either. I sure am not going to do it for you, but I can build a capable boat and play like I would if I want to.

I have made three trips so far. The first time, I went by myself just to see how the boat worked. It is sort of outlaw rigged. For one thing, it is the first sliding-gunter rigged boat I have ever built. I make a fetish of a big sail area with spars short enough to stow in the boat, and the simplest way I have found to do that is a sprit-rig with the sprit and mast the same length. Such a thing is hard to reef while you are in the boat, though. The way I have been working it is to snatch down the sprit when it breezes up and limp ashore with the peak of the sail flopping on the lee side ("scandalized") so that I can stagger all around the boat to put in a proper reef. The rocky places where I will go in this little boat aren't conducive to this kind of fooling around, though. My collaboration with Stuart Hopkins (*Dabbler Sails*) convinced me that a full-battened, Rushton-style bat wing canoe sail is the trick and he was right. This sail is eighty-five square feet with a mast just barely able to stow from stem to post, but with the yard and boom considerably shorter. Reefing is so quick that the time the boat is luffing is too short for it to drift back on one of the close together oyster bars I have been working in. One cute trick when close hauled is to snatch the halyard loose, drop the butt of the yard to the thwart, catch the top horizontal batten with my hand, and using that grip as the sheet, ease, close hauled almost dead upwind to the landing place without having to luff up or leave the tiller. Which, that's another peculiarity . . . the tiller. For one thing, it has an extension that screws on with a take-down pool cue joint. This extension is used when there is only one person in the boat. There is a gaff hook that screws on the extension handle in case I catch a big cobio. They like to hang around crab traps and things. They are picky eaters but don't know what to make of a cast net—ain't got no destructive teeth, so they can't bite a hole in it, and they are big enough to cut into steaks and cook on the grill. Of course, some of them are so big that it might be a contest of who caught whom.

The places I like to fish are places nobody in their right mind would go. The Apalachee Bay shoreline is so convoluted with little creeks and bays that it's actually hundreds of miles longer than it looks like it is. The only trouble is that most of the places are so shallow, rocky, and full of oyster bars that it is dangerous to get out of the channel. Even a Jet Ski don't like too many oyster shells in the impeller, and such shallow water is certainly no place for an outboard motor. If you know where you are and have a very light boat, the shoreline between Apalachicola and Crystal River is a fascinating place. A little, light sailboat works best for us, but it has to have a good retractable rudder. This one works by a little cable to the tiller. Pushing down on the tiller pulls the rudder blade down, and when it comes time to cross a bar, a lift of the tiller lets the rudder float up and decreases the draft of the boat instantly to three or four inches. The rudder is balanced with a good bit of blade ahead of the gudgeon holes when it is down. That lets it act like a keel so it pulls the center of lateral resistance back and you can feel it eliminate the weather helm when you push it down. One hand on the tiller, the other on the dagger board . . . the sheet in the teeth . . . look out, chickens, here I come.

Another peculiarity is the auxiliary propulsion. It is essential in places like that for the boat to be as light as possible so it can be carried or dragged with all its gear. Oars are heavy, so this boat is made to be paddled. It is a strange rig. When I am by myself and there is no wind, I pole or paddle with a long, light (six feet, twelve ounces) paddle while I am standing up straddling the spars and sail. When I am with my wife or one of these children, I slip the spars over the stern until the heel of the mast will go under the bow thwart (way up front over the mast step). That frees up the thwart so my wife can perch up there and paddle with a double paddle. I push the head of the mast and the sail off to port and sit on the starboard side of the stern thwart and steer (I tried to paddle, but my wife is so effective with that double paddle in the bow that I wasn't accomplishing anything but drag and confusion).

The spars are all hollow, octagonal, tapered both in diameter and wall thickness and very light. The whole bundle—mast (11'8" long × 2¼" dia. × 19 oz.), yard, boom, sail, rigging, and cover—weighs only five and a half pounds. The double paddle and the stand-up stern paddle are also hollow-octagonal and all. The stand-up paddle, as an experiment, has a wall thickness that tapers to only 1/16-inch at the shank down by the blade and up by the knob—ain't broke it yet. The double paddle is a reject where I tried to brand the logo onto the wood after it was fiberglassed and made something that looks like the tattoo on the first naked woman I ever saw in my life (down on State Street in Chicago while I was in boot camp. I was country come to town).

Another weird thing is the dagger board, and there is more than one weird thing about it. For one, the case just sticks up in the middle of the boat through the floorboards without any visible means of support. It ain't but eight inches wide, so one of us can straddle it as we sit in the bottom of the boat (the usual sailing position). I found out a long time ago that it takes a lot less to break a dagger board off (I have a spare) than it does to hurt the case if it is just glued to the bottom and the two sawn floor "timbers" fore and aft of it. On the bottom of the boat there are our usual little Bernoulli-principle venturi bumps alongside the slot to pull the water out of the case. It works well. When you are running downwind with the dagger board out, you can see the water run out of the case when the boat begins to move. When a boat is towed at planing speed, air is sucked out of the slot and makes a white streak in the water like the exhaust wake of an outboard motor. I would put a drain plug in there to bail the boat, but our dagger boards are so thin (5/16-inch quarter-sawn, epoxy-fiberglassed ash) that it would have to be too little to do any good. The dagger board also pivots fore and aft to adjust the center of lateral resistance. I don't like an out-of-balance boat with a hard weather helm. A rudder dragging hard-over in the water ruins upwind performance worse than most anything. Some little light boats don't like to come about into a head chop if they are balanced without weather helm, though. Just a tweak on the pivoting dagger board swings the tip forward about two feet to make this boat snap right around. As a matter of fact, I have never sailed a boat that will quick-tack like this. I guess an Optimist pram or a Nutshell might do it as quickly. The fully battened sail seems never to stop working. There is no true backwinding of the luff at all, just a little ripple as the bow passes through the eye of the wind, then the battens pop over and the boat is boogying along on the other tack. It almost seems as if, when the battens snap to the other side, they flip the fabric enough to give a little extra push, but that's probably just my imagination. Whatever it is, the boat doesn't even quit sizzling when it whips over. It just instantly crosses the wind.

The first trip was to the old St. Marks river mouth. The tide is stiff up there in the bight (for Florida) and there is always a strong current. Everything worked so well that I was sailing up in the nooks of the bars to get as much as I could with each tack. I would tack just at the last minute before the dagger board bit the rocks. I beat up the river with the tide (ain't nothing like three or four knots of help to make windward work go quick). When I got to the straight stretch before the confluence of the St. Marks and Wakulla rivers, I latched her down to make my sardine sandwich. Just about the time I got my bread laid out on the thwart and was peeling my onion, a pushboat with two empty barges came out of the St. Marks River from the power plant pushing a wall of water against that tide. I had to slip over behind a bar, out of the current, and heave to to get away from him in that narrow channel. There I made another discovery and my sandwich, too. The little boat hoves up so neatly. It never actually falls off the wind enough to move. I guess it is the way those battens hold the belly in the sail. When it luffs up, it only stays there a second or two before dropping off, and it doesn't fall off but just the tiniest little bit. It is hard to see that it does anything but sit stationary. I was in a narrow little place and the boat just laid to for ten minutes while that tow passed. I couldn't tell that I moved at all, not even when the wake went under us—pretty good little gusty breeze of wind, too. It is really unusual in that respect, particularly for a keel-less, dagger board rig.

After I ate my lunch, I dipped up a handful of water and rinsed the mustard out of my stubbles, pulled the dagger board out, eased the sheet, fell off downwind, and turned up into the tide behind the tug. I passed him, too. I could hear those two puny little out-of-synch 16-V-71s bleating like the barges were aground as I wove back and forth in the shallows between the bars, manipulating my retracting rudder like an ace to stay out of the current. I could see the redfish (red drum) on the bottom as I tore past. I had debated about maybe tying that last line of reef points because it was breezy and I didn't know what the boat would act like going dead downwind. I sure didn't want to have to do anything wild in that little maze of short water and sharp rocks and oysters out of the channel, but again, there was nothing to worry about. Though I had my lizard on the rail ready to vang the boom down, something, either those battens or my slightly aft-of-the-mast gooseneck downhaul, kept the boom from lifting and yawing the boat. Stuart's cut of the panels might have had something to do with it. Maybe, since there is no way to snatch much bias, they can't work up enough elasticity together to lift the boom in any kind of synchronous way. Anyway, not only did it boil along dead downwind without trying to yaw at all, the head of the sail didn't twist. I pulled the dagger board out and let the rudder trail and whipped all between those fishing boats and bars like a ricochet. Sometimes the water was so shallow I could hear the oyster shells rumble under me from the disturbance of my passing. When I sailed by one big anchored boat with fifteen thousand bucks worth of outboard motors on the stern, I heard one fisherman say to the other, "You know he just went by heading up the river . . . now here he comes back. . . . How the hell he do that? Ain't got room for no motor. Look at him . . . sitting right there in the damn bottom of the boat. . . . Old man, too . . . must be some kinda Yankee not to know you cain't go up in there where he at in no boat."

The next trip was the day before Thanksgiving. My wife was off from school and we went to St. Marks early. Since the wind was NE (one reef's worth) and the tide was rising, we decided to beat up the river, catch a few fish just before the turn of the tide, and fly back out with a fair wind and a fair tide. We messed around the bars of the river until we found a good-looking one where we got out and ate our lunch. About halfway through I heard a mullet jump, so I got my net and made one throw. The net was full of fish as I pulled it in, and in the clear water, I could see a small shovel-nosed (bonnet-head) shark just before he cut out. I also saw some mullet run out the hole after him and the flash of at least two redfish. I was mortified until I realized that something was still snatching in there . . . five big sheepheads, one of my favorite fish. I already told you about how to poach them for salad and soup, but you can fry them, too. The fillets fit the pan just so and lie flat. And you can save the heads for soup. By the time we got loaded up to go, the tide had turned. We swept down the river like Beelzebub was on our tail. When we got to the mouth of the little dredged channel that leads to the Federal Wildlife Refuge boat ramp, some dog flies came in the boat with us. I had intended to beat up the narrow channel to the ramp just to be cute, but before I had made the first short-tack, my wife had dropped the sail, snatched the mast out of the hole, planted her stern in its place, and was capably attacking the water with the double paddle. She does not like to be eaten up by dog flies and it was all I could do to hang on back there in the stern. Though it was a no-wake zone, she was rolling the fiddler crabs off the mud up into the grass. In case you don't know, dog flies look just like houseflies but instead of that little foot-looking thing on their proboscis, they have something that works just like a power-driven square mortising chisel. They are just as smart and hard to kill as a regular fly, but they bite like something blowed off a cutting torch and they are relentless. I ain't real crazy about them myself.

The next trip was the day after Thanksgiving. The crowd had et up all my sheepheads but I had the hole in my net tied back up and was determined to catch enough fish to tide us over until my wife sent her schoolchildren home for Christmas break. Usually I can catch a few freshwater fish right near the shop, but the drought was so bad (worst since 1957) that all my little honey holes were dried up and I had to go to the coast. We took off early and, when we put in, the tide was falling against us. I made a few fancy little short tacks in between the bars trying to get up the river to one of my low-tide holes, but, though it was fun, we were swimming in the same place the whole time. My wife, without a word, dropped the sail, pulled the mast out of the hole, planted her stern where it had been, and began to attack the water with that double paddle (don't ever let an independent-minded woman get hold of a double paddle if you really don't want to go somewhere is my advice). Pretty soon we were way back in the wonderful maze of oyster bars, shallow water, and deep holes east of the main channel (called "East River" on the chart). I caught six mullet, two big redfish, and three speckled trout (spotted weakfish, squeteague) before I caught me another sheephead—all that in two throws of the net. I turned all but one of the redfish and two red-roe (gravid female) mullet loose. I kept them and my sheephead. If you don't believe fried red-roe is good to eat, give a banana-sized piece to a baby . . . then send him (or her) home to her (or his) momma.

We loaded up our fish, washed the mud off our feet and shanks, hoisted our beautiful little sail, and made such a sight sailing quietly out of the marsh that a good photographer would have jumped for the camera. Of course, no photographer or anybody else was within miles of us, but I wondered what our little rig looked like easing along in the beautiful afternoon light.

No sailboat, no matter how wonderfully it is shaped, how elegantly it is built, how lightly it floats, or how perfectly balanced the rig will do a damned thing with a bad sail. A long time ago, for my own boats, I used to try to make my own sails to save a little money. I used cheap cloth and very little talent and they turned out looking sort of like a rump-sprung skirt. I have always insisted that my customers get their sails from somebody who knows what he is doing. I insist that I have the sail (most of my boats only have one sail) in hand before I will rig the boat. Sailmaking is a tricky business and there are a lot of people who can do it pretty good, but some make it an art.

The sail sets beautifully in all conditions. It is an heirloom. There is never a wrinkle anywhere. The peak does not wash out to leeward at all, either close hauled or off the wind, reefed or all-up. The airfoil stays perfect under all conditions. It has the same shape as a pelican's wing—a wonderful thing to fly through the sky. Stuart Hopkins and I decided to make the sail out of the lightest possible Dacron, 2.5 ounces, the same as for an Optimist pram. I know it was hard to keep that light fabric straight under the needle for every one of those battens, but it was worth it. I think that's why it flies in the air so well. When the sail is reefed, the battens keep it straight, and because of that and the lightweight cloth, the bundle at the bottom is very small and there is no naked mast sticking up above the peak. I know that helps the windward performance of such a small boat. There are two epoxified and fiberglassed octagonal wood cylinders (they look like wood coffee cups) that slide on the mast and carry the yard. I call it a Stuart Hopkins rig. The top cup has a hook that engages rigidly to the yard. This cylinder is the attachment point for the halyard. The other coffee cup pivots at the heel of the yard, holding it straight with the mast. The yard slides up and down the mast like it was greased and stays right at both reef points without having to fool around with double halyards. Because the two cylinders are attached rigidly to the yard, it stays lined up with the mast, just so, even in gusts . . . follows the sail around exactly. I fudged the mast a little bit to anticipate the back-bend, so it has an easy-to-see curve toward the bow when it is sitting still. I even had sense enough to mark the front and back by using one of the sides of the octagon with a little sapwood to show the front. Too bad I didn't put it at the bottom where I could see it.

To wrap it up (finally). The little boat is better than I ever hoped. It is fast, stable, and weatherly, easy to sail, quickest to rig, reef, and tack that I ever saw. It is even dry. I hoped it would be because I have built that kind of bow on skiffs before. It doesn't seem logical to some, but a wide bow does better if it only has a little hollow just at the forefoot, not all the way up the side in a "flare" to peel the water up high so that it blows back in the boat. That might work for boats that are big enough to hide behind, but with little boats, it is best to hit the waves with something convex so that the bow sort of foams through instead of cutting up a hell of a sheet. This is the bluffest bowed sailboat I have built, though, and a side effect that I hadn't anticipated is the sound of it. It sort of makes a rushing, roaring noise, not the lapping, slapping sound of a sharp lap-strake bow. When it is going good and the sail is pushing the bow down and I slide back to keep the sheet from lifting the stern, everything gets very steady and the roaring up there sounds mighty good. Reaching or on the wind, she just lays one of those fat cheeks down on the water and snoozes. It ain't hard to look at that bluff bow forging ahead and see myself in a sixteenth-century ship's boat in the middle of the endless wilderness. Dang, I wish I didn't have all this work to do. But I do *need* to go back down there to check on my chickens.

Crackers and Cheese (a poem)

Squatting on an oyster bar.
Eating crackers and cheese.
Thick crust of mud.
On both my knees.

Thought I heard a mullet.
He went ker-ploop.
"Hold it, Jane.
Let's wait.
On that soup."

Scrambled for my net.
Skipping over the bar.
Saw a little flash.
Not too far.

Net spun out.
With nary a fold.
Shovel-nosed shark.
Bit such a hole.

The mullet got out.
So did some reds.
Caught five, though.
All sheepheads.

THE CARIBS AND THE ARAWAKS

in which I figure out economics,
but too late to participate in any of it

I AM BUILDING A big deal rowboat. It is sixteen feet long and six feet wide . . . rows ten foot, Sitka spruce, Shaw & Tenney (the oldest oar makers in this country) oars, and its primary use will be for exercise. Besides rowboats, I build little sailboats, extra-light paddling boats, small inboard or outboard skiffs, and combination rigs to serve as yacht tenders and camp cruisers. Through the forty years I have been building boats, enough people have found out about me that if I accepted deposits from everyone who wants me to build them a boat, inflation would become a factor in the deal before I could get around to the job.

I had my tax consultation with my CPA daughter-in-law, a redheaded woman of few words and no tolerance for foolishness. I asked her why, since I had more work than I could do and I kept going up and up on the price, I still wasn't making no money. She explained that even if you double nothing, you still just have nothing. "But what about the law of supply and demand?" I whined. "That only works if you can buckle down to supply enough of that demand to make a little money," said she. "Well, I might as well just go to the coast," said me. "Yep," was her final word.

So I have reversed the bidding process. Now the customer tells me what he (or she . . . there have been a few . . . one was a bona-fide rocket scientist) wants and what it is worth to her and I accept the most tempting offer when the new boat goes out the door. It is not always just the money that tempts me. If I loved money, I would have given this foolishness up long, long ago. An offer to get me to build almost any kind of small sailboat is more tempting than anything else (which, as an aside, I think a sailboat is certainly the most wonderful invention of mankind), but there is a time when these big deal exercise rowboats (I call them "bull market skiffs") kind of edge them out. Though I don't love money, I am very fond of the freedom to mess around in my own little boats that a little wad enables, and the buyers of these kinds of rowboats are apt get their way with me by waving a *big* wad.

There is a time when some people will buy a boat even when they don't actually have any use for one. I think it is that they have so much money that they can't think of anything else to buy—like when the bull lets them hold a big pile. They know they need some exercise and their dignity won't let them go out and trot up and down the road where their peers can see just how out of shape they are as they strut smugly past in their big, shiny Exhibitions, so these sedentary rich people decide to top it the knob in a "designer boat . . . something with a lot of nice wood" so people will know that they are *somebody* while they are exercising instead of being mistaken for just some sloppy beer drinker in a hurry to get back to the trailer.

Maybe there is more to the self-indulgences of both those tycoons and me than just saying, "I got enough money to get this man to build anything I want." Or "I'll go to the coast until this little wad finishes dwindling the rest of the way away." Maybe neither of us has any business being so arrogant. Back in the thirties, my father got all deep into the pre-Columbian history of the Antilles. He was a good researcher and managed to dig up all sorts of interesting stuff from the remnants, and what he figured out was that there were two main groups of people in those islands—the Caribs and the Arawaks—and the Caribs were raising those Arawaks like free-range livestock. They were absentee ranchers, too, and didn't even live on their farms. They stayed down around Venezuela most of the time. They must have kept books or something, because they worked their stock in systematic cycles. They checked on each island about every twenty years or so. I guess they would look in the book and say, "Dang, it's about time to go see what's happening up there on Fat Cat Cay." Then they would pile in the long, swift canoe and paddle up there and take everything those Arawaks on that island had accumulated since the last visit. Then they would have a big barbecue and eat up some of the young, plump Arawaks. Of course, they would tie up a few to throw in the bottom of the boat to haul back to the main outfit for the homecoming festivities.

I hope the cannibals didn't eat the man of the rowboat I am building now. He was calling me about twice a week to check on the progress of the piddling and he came a few times in an SUV as big as a UPS truck to stand around in my little shop and ask questions. He was a nice man. He hadn't been around boats or shops much—more an office type of person—and could stand a little more exercise. At least all his childhood curiosity hadn't deteriorated completely. I was getting to where I liked him and loved explaining things to him. I was planning to tell him all about the Caribs and the Arawaks next time I saw him. I knew he would be interested, but I haven't heard a word from that man for a long time.

I think that a division of labor that evolved for maybe fifteen or twenty thousand years is part of mankind . . . our role might be written in our DNA. Of course, the real Caribs and Arawaks with their direct ways are long gone, but I bet that system is still working. I think that Mr. Exxon and Mr. Enron and people like that are the modern Caribs. Us old fat-cat Arawaks just think all this stuff belongs to us . . . that we are in control of this good life that is so much more satisfactory than the hunting, fishing, and gardening we evolved to do. We think we are accumulating and consuming stuff and taking medicine and living and working and paying the bills longer just because "we are worth it." We are worth it all right, but not to ourselves. I think it is paying off for them Caribs. There is a correlation between that Friday when the Dow and the Nasdaq fell like that and the last time I heard from my man. I hope Mike Rosoff didn't send a boatload of cannibals up here to round his plump ass up, but if they did, I know just what I'll do. I'll have a dagger board case and mast step in this skiff before you could say "Liberian tanker" and the rudder gudgeons on the stern before you could say "pre-approved."

AN ANALOG MIND STUCK IN A DIGITAL WORLD

in which I finally, in the twilight of my life, figure out what the hell is wrong with me and effect a complete cure

I WAS STARTING TO think that I was going to turn out to be one of those disgruntled old men who snap at everybody. I wasn't paying attention to what the people in my family were saying anymore. It was getting to where my own opinions were taking on far more importance than at any other time since I started trying to get over puberty. I listened to a radio show on NPR where they explained that cheerfulness was healthy. As soon as I started on my cheerfulness program to regain my youth, I noticed that my grandchildren stopped playing with me. It took a trip into the bathroom to explain why. We had all taught the children not to play with people with such a leer as the one I saw in the mirror in there. I let my face fall into the normal wattles and wrinkles that it has accumulated over the years. Everybody seemed relieved except me. I decided to stop drinking.

I am not a hard drinker, mind you—I'm not the type to try to suck the bottom out of the bottle and then raise hell all over the place, but I do like to clutch my old trusty glass and prop up my feet on time every evening. It seems that the older I get, the more important this little ritual becomes. Since the search for the reason why I was getting to be so disagreeable hadn't turned up anything else yet, I decided that maybe, at this late stage in my life, I was deluding myself about my little habit. Maybe, I told myself, it is a big habit and it is ruining your life. I stopped completely for a long time. It was a help in some ways. I found that I could tie enough flies to keep ahead of the ones I popped off my line or hung up in the top limbs of trees because of the time I saved when my feet weren't propped up, but I remained just as grumpy as ever. It began to interfere with the exercise of my authority, sort of like with the boy who cried "Wolf." The grandchildren began to ignore instructions that I issued in my best stern voice. I realized that it was because I always sound like that now. It is hard to pay attention when an old man grumbles because you are standing on his belly in hard shoes, when the way he sounds is the same as when you are standing on his belly not in hard shoes. Luckily, just as I was reaching the end of my rope, I discovered the real reason and was able to correct the problem.

It was the damned clocks. All of our clocks were the new digital style and they were all over the place. The radio had one, the car had one (actually two, one on its aftermarket radio and this crazy damned thing on the dashboard that came with it when it was new . . . I guess) and there was one on each of the bedside tables where my wife and I sleep. There were two in my shop: one on the radio in there and one on the time clock where my employee used to punch his card before he punched out because I was getting so hard to get along with. Everywhere you looked, they were smugly displaying numerals . . . digits . . . 11:11 . . . things like that . . . 1:23 . . . for Christ's sake . . . 12:21 . . . as if that had some significance.

I was waiting in line at the post office to try to buy some stamps because the machine in the lobby refused to respond to some pretty hard licks and strong language. In the line, a nice old lady was trying to find out what time it was from a nice young girl ahead of me. "Ten fifty-nine," was the reply. The old lady seemed a little hard of hearing and asked again. "TEN FIFTY-NINE," was the reply. She still didn't understand, "IT'S TEN FIFTY-NINE," hollered the girl. "Why don't you just say it's almost eleven o'clock," I suggested. "Well, it is now," said the girl. "Eleven zero zero." I looked at my watch, an old self-winding Bulova that has been keeping perfect time for years and years. I saw that it was not quite eleven yet. The long hand was almost there but not quite. I took issue with the girl about the precise way in which she was mistaken. She smugly pointed at the satellite adjusted electronic clock on the machine on the postmaster's counter . . . 11:00:41 . . . 42 . . . 43 . . . official government time. I was embarrassed.

Confrontations like that were not the cause of my irritable nature, but a result of it. There used to be a time when I was almost obsequious with such young women and accepted whatever time they said with good cheer. It was just the digital nature of the information that was getting to me. The poisonous seeds of digital irritation were being planted every night and manured and watered all day long every time I saw one of those damned clocks.

I always wake up two or three times each night to see what time it is. It is an old habit left over from years of standing watches on boats at sea. I half wake up, look at the clock, and then roll over and mumble to myself, "Hot dog, it ain't but about ten o'clock, let me snuggle back down here right this minute." Or, "Goody, goody, I still got about an hour and a half before the alarm goes off, let me droop back off 'til then." Or, "Still got a little more than a half an hour, oh joy, I thought it was later than that, think I'll snooze just a short little snort or two more." Then one of the children kicked the last of the old Baby Bens off the stool and busted the smithereens out of it so badly that even I couldn't get them to goagulate back in there again.

We bought a digital clock radio. At first I thought that the thing that was irritating me was the ridiculous, cartoon-character-sounding voice of the announcer of the radio station first thing every morning. I soon learned to circumvent that and then I thought it was the backhoe-in-reverse sound of the electronic alarm that was grating on my last nerve. So I went to the store and made the poor harassed-seeming clerk plug in all the clock radios they had until I found one that just made a loud buzzing sound like a seventeen-year-old cicada in a beer can, which, for some reason, did not irritate me too bad. I put the other radio on my wife's side so she could see what time it was on her own clock without having to crawl all over me to get a myopic glimpse at mine. That was another sign of the degeneration of my good nature, that this now irritated me after all those years.

Time (5:55) to bring this to a close. The truth dawned on me one night when I woke up, looked at the clock, and flew off into a rage right there in the bed, "3:21? What you mean, 3:21, you damn fool you? What kind of countdown is that? You with that dead-looking battery hanging out on that little wire. You think you so modern . . . you got a face like a 1950 Mercury." Luckily my wife got me calmed back down before I electrocuted myself. The trouble was that I don't have enough sense, in the middle of the night, to figure out what "4:44" means. I have to wake completely up and do the fool arithmetic. I have always hated arithmetic. The only way I got through school was by memorizing, estimating, and my momma's politicking. The mere sight of digits like 2:02 reminds me of past failure and, in the middle of the night, kills the joy of the time left.

I unplugged every one of the blinking things and had a yard sale. I was able to make enough money off it to buy an old Big Ben and a Baby Ben, two old surplus schoolhouse clocks, a roll of black plastic tape to cover up both the 11:11's and 10:01's in the car and still had enough left to get my old Bulova cleaned. Now all I have to do is keep my mouth closed in the post office, and that's not nearly as much trouble as it was. If I could just find some good store-bought flies everything would be all right. "Just look at these hooks . . . wire big enough to make eyeglass frames with. How in the world is a man supposed to get a thing like that to float? Seems like for all that money they could make one that didn't have the hook sticking out to the side like a dog raising his leg. Holy mackerel, child, get off my belly with those big clodhop cowboy boots, you gonna make me spill my drink."

COOKING UP OPINIONS

*in which I finally set aside my peculiar ways and start
acting like all the other old men in the world*

As a boatbuilder I ought to go to boat shows more, but I can't stand it. Boat shows are hotbeds for the sprouting of opinions. The older I get, the more fond I become of my own and the less delighted I am with those of others. What happens is that when people start telling me their opinions, I find that I am backing up. I try to control it by consciously taking steps forward, but the net result is that I just keep backing toward the clearing until I just ain't around anymore.

I have more opinions of my own, too, now that I am getting old (hold on just a minute while I turn Paul Harvey off). I thought it was the result of my solitary profession. Fiddling around in the seclusion of my shop, planing, scraping, sanding, and painting are the sorts of things that free up the mind and foster the growth of opinions. I was so tickled with myself that I decided to share my views. Back when

I used to have employees and apprentices, I would explain while the work was actually going on. After they all left my employ in search of other ways to become upwardly mobile, I had to find another outlet for the distribution of my opinions.

I began by offering them up to prospective boat customers. At first I confined my little speeches to boat design and construction (a rich field). Someone would come to the shop to have a look at the boat in the works. "I see you have just a bit of tumblehome back by the stern," one man said. "Yes, I like tumblehome. It gives a good convexity to the topsides and curvature to the rails, which strengthens the whole boat," I said. Then I began to explain the history of tumblehome, how tumbling home the topsides made a clear run from the hounds to the chainplates for the shrouds of old ships and how tumblehome saved the poorly supported bulwarks of ships by presenting the ends of the strong deck beams to the impact of the ship with the dock. By the time I got to the part where, in small sailboats, tumblehome keeps the rails from scooping up water into the boat when it heels, I noticed that I could no longer clearly see the pupils of that man's eyes. At first I thought there was something wrong with me, but then I realized that there was something wrong with him. I knew I had to try to give my opinions a wider range. I decided to write them down and send them off. Coincidentally, the boat business began to fall off and that gave me time to type.

After I had refined the crop on hand and sent them off for consideration for publication by all sorts of magazines and literary journals, I sat back down at the typewriter so as to be ready when the new opinion crop sprouted. I sat there for a long time before I realized that the ground was barren. I began to fear that I might not be able to become the Will Rogers of the new millennium. I was heartbroken. I couldn't understand it until I, fortunately, finally, received a commission for a new boat. As soon as I started, the font of opinion began to flow again. I was delighted. Then I found my aluminum hard hat.

It is funny how you can lose a thing like that and have it turn up right there in plain sight. My granddaughters had fixed it up as a dog watering dish, and I guess I just got used to it sitting over in the corner by the drinking fountain. Wouldn't have noticed it at all except that while I was getting a drink, I elbowed my teeth off the edge of the cooler where I keep them handy in case a customer was to show up. They went "ploop" right in dog water in the hard hat. I used that hard hat, not to protect my head from bumps, but to shield it from the heat lamps that I use to facilitate the penetration of the epoxy. I heat-sheathe all the planks with fiberglass and epoxy in a secret way before they go on the boat, so I have to spend a lot of time with my head under the heat lamps while I spread the epoxy onto the fiberglass with a little plastic squeegee. The aluminum hard hat kept the infrared light from cooking my brains. After I lost the hat, I found that epoxy spreading was very stimulating to the opinion-forming process.

When I found it and started using it again, the opinion mill slowed down. You guessed it. Vast experience and natural brilliance were not the cause of the phenomenon at all. It was the heat of the lamps soaking through my skull and boiling up these opinions out of the depths—sort of like how the oil comes out of an old piece of cheese when you leave it out on the seat of the boat in the hot sun. It probably wasn't good for me. It never is good to push a tool beyond its normal capacity. Power tools will do a little more if you force them, but after a while, they'll get hot and start stinking. Which, I believe I smell hair burning right now.

ACKNOWLEDGMENTS

FIRST I WANT to thank my family and friends, either living or dead, happy or sad, glad or mad. Those of you who ain't dead yet know who you are and how pitifully you have been used by me, and I appreciate it.

Next, I want to thank all the editors who have published my stuff in the past . . . this won't take long: Jim Doherty and Judy Rice, who used to be at *Smithsonian* and *Natural History*, respectively . . . before Martha Stewart or whoever it was bought those magazines away from their museums and gave my good editors their walking papers. There is Matt Murphy, Peter Spectre, and Tom Jackson at *Woodenboat*. Peter Spectre is also editor of *Maine Boats and Harbors* and so is Gretchen Piston Ogden. These are the kinds of people who are unafraid of risks, undaunted by problems, and . . . few and far between. Then there is Bob Hicks, who, with his family, publishes the remarkable *Messing About in Boats* every two weeks. *Messing* has printed more of my gibberish than all others (including this book) combined. Without the enthusiastic approval of Bob and his subscribers, the messers, I wouldn't have near as much nerve as I do now. Peternelle van Arsdale is the editor of this book. One of the reasons that I have become an old man without attaining great fame and fortune is because I am sort of intolerant of too much interference with my foibles and I have to tell you that I was kind of worried when this thing flopped on Peternelle's desk in New York City. Hell, I have snatched thousands of dollars worth of literature, smack, like a lollypop, from the lips of presumptuous editors. Good editing is not only a ticklish business, but an art, and Peternelle has it down to a science.

Then there is my agent, John Silbersack. He read some of my nonsense somewhere and wrote to ask me if I had enough for a book. I sent him about seventy-five pounds of paper like what I had been trying to sell for about fifty years. He culled out this little bit and . . . sold it. What talent.